OLD ENGLISH FURNITURE

PLATE I

QUEEN CHARLOTTE WITH TWO OF HER SONS, THE PRINCE OF WALES AND DUKE OF YORK

From the painting by Johann Zoffany, R.A., by gracious permission of H.M. The King.

Painted about 1767, this picture shows the charming dressing-table treatment of the period.

THERLE HUGHES

OLD ENGLISH FURNITURE

LUTTERWORTH PRESS
LONDON

First published 1949
Second impression 1950

PRINTED IN GREAT BRITAIN
AT THE CHISWICK PRESS, NEW SOUTHGATE, LONDON, N.11

CONTENTS

ILLUSTRATIONS

Plate *Facing page*

1

INTRODUCTION

TO acquire an antique is to recapture a fragment of a vanished world. And of all antiques none is more satisfying, because none is more intimately associated with the life of that world, than a piece of household furniture. The aim of this book is to consider each of these familiar antiques, not as a museum specimen, but as a contribution to the everyday life of those who first made or used it. Only thus is it possible to appreciate the underlying reasons for each development, the structural necessities and the vagaries of fashion governing the products, not only of the great "names" in furniture creation, but of the many lesser men who built up this country's magnificent reputation for honest craftsmanship.

Most people approach a book such as this with personal problems regarding specific pieces of furniture, and for this reason the natural evolution of each article has been traced separately. In this way the important periods in its development are made plain—and not only dead dates but something of the urgent, restless life that found expression in such creative effort. But it must be stressed that in reality all these pieces were interrelated and at the same time dependent upon a natural, haphazard dispersion of ideas that might make individual craftsmen ten, twenty, or fifty years ahead or behind in material and method. Dates given in this book must be taken as approximate and in general applying to London work.

The ideas themselves originated largely on the Continent —Italy, France, the Netherlands, Germany, Spain—and even in India and the Far East. It has always been typical of this country to seek and welcome foreign ways, and then so to adapt them to our own high standards that the homely results evolved have a wholly native charm and supply a faithful index to the manners, tastes, and personalities of the men and women whose daily lives they served.

Such gradual changes do not fit easily into the crude divisions of centuries or monarchies; but for the sake of clarity the following summary may be taken to indicate the general trends among the leaders in furniture design, and the distinctive styles that characterized those vanished days, expressed in a thousand details of design, material, and ornament.

For this purpose the *medieval period* covers the decorative styles of the "Early English" and "Decorated" Gothic (1200-1280 and 1280-1370), and the simpler "Perpendicular" Gothic which evolved after the enormous havoc of the Black Death in the mid-fourteenth century and particularly affected furniture forms. Some room panelling was in use by the thirteenth century and the Close Rolls of Henry III refer to walls painted in imitation of the early Continental tapestries. But the average furniture used in a feudal settlement consisted of a very few bare necessities. These articles were mainly chests, tables, benches, stools, and a few turned chairs; their material was mainly oak and whatever other native woods happened to be available. In their construction these pieces showed planks which were thicker towards one edge than the other, and to appreciate this early work it is necessary to know something of the way the oak was handled.

The earliest method was to split the felled tree with a rivening tool, following the natural growth-formation lines of cleavage in the trunk. By splitting along the lines of dense non-cellular tissue radiating from the centre of the trunk and known as medullary rays, the log was fairly easily quartered and then further divided into usable segments. It happened that the faces of these planks and scantlings displayed to the full the well-known "silver grain" of the dense tissue, but those old craftsmen had more practically discovered that this method minimized subsequent warping and twisting. Even then the wood was mellowed for many years before being used, the method of seasoning influencing the eventual colour and tone.

Later the saw replaced the old heavy hammer (or "beetle") and wedge, but for some time it continued to be the custom to quarter the trunk and saw the planks as far as possible along the old lines. (Fig. 1A shows three ways of cutting such planks.) These planks were narrower than those obtained by sawing the trunk along lines parallel with its diameter (Fig. 1B), but the wide planks reacted disconcertingly to atmospheric changes: in time oak wood becomes case hardened but never completely seasoned. The large, two-handled saw dated from the mid-sixteenth century, but it was not until after 1660 that the softer tissue of the wide planks was found to have a positive advantage in absorbing lacquer and the glues used in veneer. And by then the tough, home-grown oak was being supplemented by imported oak, softer, whiter, and more easily worked, and the "age of walnut" was beginning.

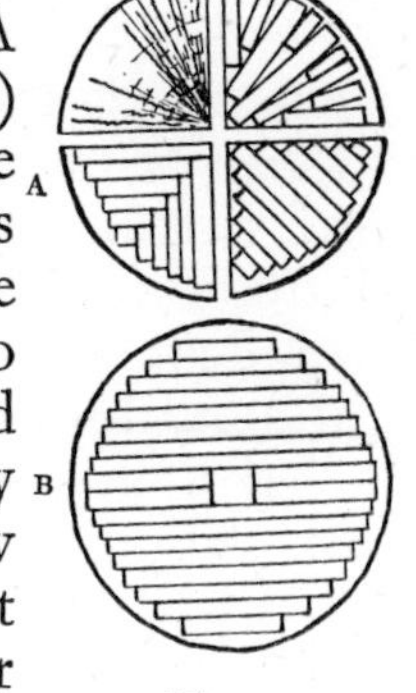

Fig. 1

The earliest methods of construction were crude, the planks being held by clout-headed nails and bands of iron; but even by the fifteenth century good quality work might show the extremely sound "framed-up" panelling and mortise-and-tenon joints which dominated furniture until the importance of construction became eclipsed by surface decoration. In such furniture as chest or box-chair the basic construction consisted of a number of wide uprights—stiles—linked by top and bottom rails and intermediate muntins to make a framework. The joints in this were formed by projections—tenons—fitting into holes—mortises—and secured by oak dowel pins driven through all three thicknesses of wood (Fig. 2). Extra firmness might be secured by the draw-bore process: the pin-hole through the tenon was made slightly out-of-line with those in the mortise walls so

Fig. 2

that as the dowel pin was driven home it drew the tenon more tightly into position. In much early furniture, too, square tapering pegs, cut from green wood, were driven into round holes. This was essentially a method of joining end-grain into side-grain, as contrasted with the end-grain into end-grain which characterized dovetailing.

This sturdy frame was so grooved that the panels, each a single piece of wood, composing the sides and ends of the chest, were held in position without nailing and thus allowed full freedom to contract and expand as atmospheric changes demanded.

Mounts throughout this period—such as key escutcheons, and handle and staple backplates (Fig. 3)—were of fine iron-work elaborately shaped, the metal cut when cold with a saw, like wood. These had considerable decorative value: although decoration of this early domestic woodwork consisted largely of vivid colour, oil paint or tempera being applied over the lime-whitened wood, metal also was extremely important. Not until after 1400 did the wood-carver's efforts begin to dominate those of the iron-worker, and for another two centuries he used the stone-mason's flutes, facets, and arches in his work. There is reason to doubt the authenticity of much so-called Gothic wood-carving, but undoubtedly some carving was introduced on wooden furniture as well as in the structure of the medieval home during this great period of ecclesiastical wood-work. A little of what remains reflects something of the richly imaginative "curvilinear" Gothic forms of the period before the Black Death (Fig. 4 is from a thirteenth-century chest) but more recalls the modified "Perpendicular" Gothic (Fig. 5) which in its turn was supplanted by round-arched Italian Renaissance styles in the sixteenth century.

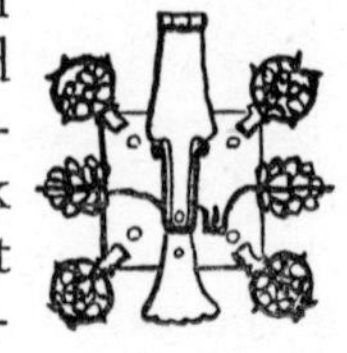
Fig. 3

Fig. 4

Fig. 5

The *early Tudor period* covered the years 1485-1558. Furniture was still nearly all made for the wealthy minority by whom many foreign workers were employed—Italian, Flemish, and German. The great increase in secular workers which resulted from Henry VIII's suppression of the monasteries contributed somewhat to more comfort in the average home. Many great houses had their walls enriched with tapestries, but the furniture in common use still consisted of a few necessities, the material principally oak, the construction sound and heavy, even the decoration largely restricted to such functional work as the various linenfold panels primarily designed to prevent warping.

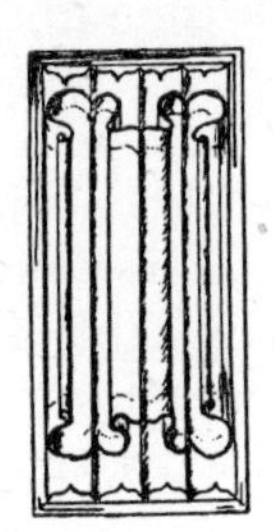
Fig. 6

At its simplest, the linenfold was carved to represent hanging fabric (Fig. 6); elaborate versions introduced fringes and tassels. The more ornate repetitive curved rib formed by two ogees set back to back—the parchemin panel—was an early sixteenth-century development (Fig. 7). These are regarded as late Gothic in character, as contrasted with the first hints at English Renaissance decoration incorporated in the Gothic forms before the latter were consciously rejected. Characteristic of the new style were the Italian arabesques and "Romagne" carved heads in medallions of Henry VIII's reign, now popular with the furniture faker (Fig. 8). Before the end of the period painted furniture was going out of fashion; the bare wood might be treated with poppy or linseed oil, often reddened with alkanet root.

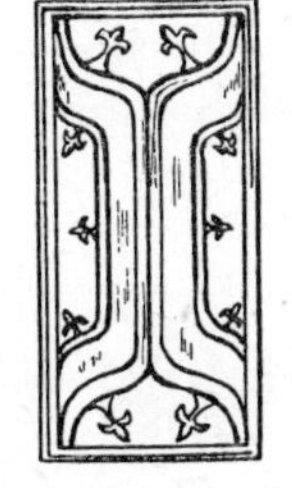
Fig. 7

The *Elizabethan period* (1558-1603) was marked by extensive building of comparatively small homes for a more cultured society and on more gracious architectural lines than had been possible in the old feudal fortress. The rooms with their wainscot panelling (wainscot from the Dutch *wagenschot*, referring to the best quality of quartered oak) and rich carving, showed a dignified mingling of classic and Gothic influence. Both panelling

Fig. 8

and ceiling were often enriched with colour and gilding. Already more foreign workmen were preparing their English fellow-craftsmen for the great influx of Continental ideas in the late seventeenth century.

The furniture of this period was still mainly for the rich, some of it imported from Flanders, but much of the rather roughly finished work was doubtless made for a new class of well-to-do master traders. Good quality articles were heavy and ornate, typified by massive wooden canopied beds and bulbous-legged tables and early court cupboards. The word cupboard had by now changed in use from open table to enclosed storage place—a small reflection of a general trend towards more personal privacy and a more civilized way of life.

The cheap, everyday material was oak but there was considerable use of solid walnut for quality work such as beds. In construction the furniture continued the well-tried methods of the previous period. In form, a general impression of great solidarity was achieved with deep carved friezes and especially with bulbous legs and columns, at their largest between 1590 and 1600. At first the central "acorn" swellings in these columns suggested the Gothic standing cup and cover (Fig. 9A); by the early seventeenth century their outlines were more pear-shaped (Fig. 9B). Drawers might be crudely dovetailed.

Fig. 9

The main decoration of this period consisted of this vigorous carving, never again so inventive or varied, and was typified at its most mature by panels suggesting the perspective of deep-set arches and by stiles carved with caryatid figures in high relief, dating from early Stuart days. Obviously much was prompted by the many pattern books then being published in the Low Countries. By the end of the period there was also rough inlaid decoration, at first in rather clumsy geometrical shapes and culminating in panels of flower-and-vase designs. The work involved cutting small pieces of contrasting woods—bog oak and holly produced popular black and white effects—and setting them into hollows cut about one-eighth of an inch deep in the solid wood of the furniture. Mounts included elaborate wrought iron hinges in various designs — plain H-shape, wedge or "butterfly", and scrolling "cock's head" (Fig. 10).

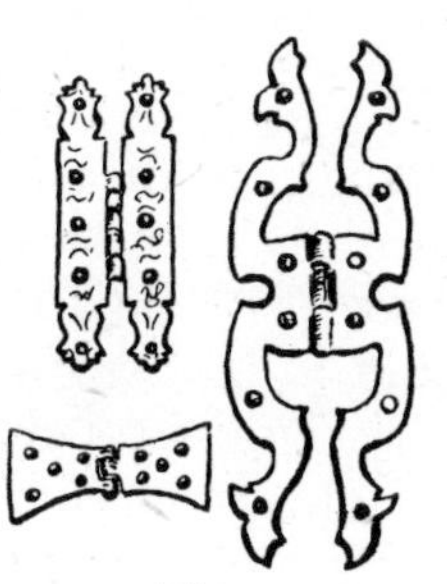

Fig. 10

The *early Stuart period* covered the reigns of James I (1603-25) and Charles I (1625-49). Picturesque Gothic work was forgotten: the increasing classicism seen in the architecture of such leaders as Inigo Jones was gradually having an effect on furniture, which developed finer profiles at the cost of the old rich carving, just as the bold melon legs gave place to typical baluster profiles. But the emphasis was still on low pieces and horizontal lines suited to the old rambling low-roomed house. An increasing demand for comfort was expressed in a little more use of upholstered furniture among the rich and an enormous supply of loose cushions and covers. In 1619 James I started the great Mortlake tapestry establishment.

Furniture innovations included more personal parlour and bedroom pieces such as the gate-leg table and tentative developments of the chest. There were more chairs, but stools were still far more numerous. The main material was oak, and the construction and form largely as before but with a greater care for such details as well-proportioned cornice mouldings. The report of a Committee of the Court of Aldermen regarding joiners' work in 1632 referred to framed, pinned, dovetailed, and glued construction, but glued furniture was largely a post-Restoration development. Dovetails gradually became smaller and closer set. Mounts included the simple loop handle in somewhat pear-shaped outline and the moulded iron drop on a shaped backplate (Fig. 11). Wooden knobs were also used.

Fig. 11

Decoration was dominated by an abundance of dull

repetitive carving such as the ancient guilloche (Fig. 12) with little depth or attempt at modelling. The Renaissance arcading was much used, a slightly raised arch being applied to the panel, but this lacked the early suggestion of depth and in late work was merely incised. Much decoration consisted of little beyond innumerable gouge cuts or lozenge-shaped incisions.

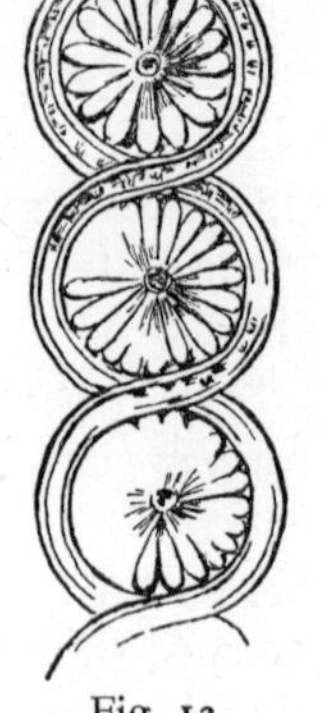
Fig. 12

The *Cromwellian period* (1649-1660) dispensed with most of this rather tasteless over-decoration and offered great opportunities, once fighting was over, for the small provincial craftsmen to produce honest work on traditional lines. New furniture included occasional bureaux, the flap hinged at the top, desk fashion. Materials were still basically oak, often treated with beeswax and turpentine, and some solid walnut. Stamped and coloured leather, which had been used for centuries on folding furniture, became popular on chairs—a Dutch adaptation of a Spanish-Moorish material. As regards form and construction, a notable feature was the quantity of turning, the dullest string-of-beads forms gradually being replaced by more interesting outlines (Fig. 13): twist-turning (Fig. 14), long practised on the Continent, was still in the experimental stage. The panels characteristic of this period projected strongly beyond the level of their stiles and rails, until they ceased to rank as panels and became meaningless glued-on decoration merely. An associated peculiarity of the late oak period, both before and after the Restoration, was the use of turned spindles and balusters, split and glued to the faces of stiles, chair uprights and so on, together with variously shaped bosses (Fig. 15 shows this on plan and in profile.) In conjunction with this Flemish trait, bolection mouldings were often

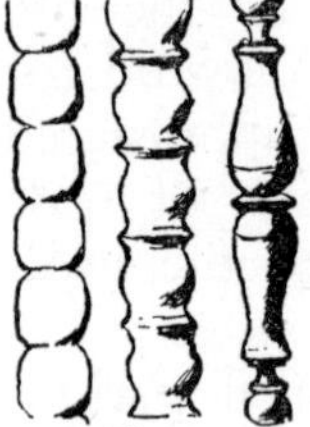
Fig. 13

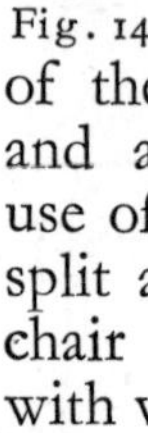

Fig. 14

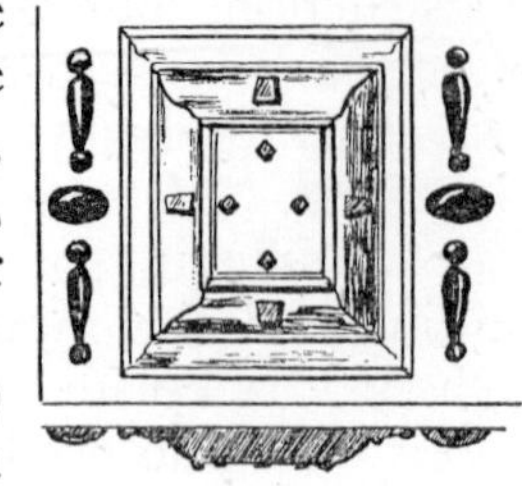
Fig. 15

applied to the flat surfaces of furniture in elaborate patterns involving many mitred corners. These treatments were used extensively around 1660: for the first time construction was masked by pseudo-functional ornament.

The *late Stuart period* may best be divided into the reigns of Charles II and James II (1660-88) and of William III and Anne (1689-1714). The year 1660 was indeed outstanding in furniture development because it was marked by the return of Charles II and his court from exile and a consequent demand for entirely new materials, designs, and workmanship, which English craftsmen could only gradually assimilate, adapt, and modify to become intrinsically English. At the same time, the great fire of 1666 led to extensive rebuilding in London in the architectural styles required of stone and brick, Renaissance architecture reaching its zenith under Wren (1632-1723) and greatly influencing the whole approach to furniture form and proportion in the following century, just as the wall carving of Grinling Gibbons (d. 1721) affected eighteenth-century furniture carving.

The main influences of the late seventeenth century were Italian, French, Dutch, Flemish, and Spanish. The effect of the East was also considerable: Charles II, impressed by all he had seen of far eastern trade in Holland, granted a charter to the East India Company, and his own wife Catherine brought him Bombay as a colourful dowry. Inventories of the period refer to various Indian fabrics, considered by some to have originated the "Jacobean" style of fabric decoration. By the end of the century the Joiners' Company was protesting indignantly that cabinet wares after English models but manufactured in the East were threatening to ruin their trade. This is thought to explain the alien touches seen in some superficially English furniture of the period.

Furniture developments included the first considerable English manufacture of mirror glass. There was much more use of upholstered furniture—often gilded or silvered to enhance elaborate carving—silks, tapestries, and needlework covers now being plentifully produced in this country. The main wood for everyday work was still oak, sometimes given an Italian flavour with pearl and ivory inlays, of which some examples have been attributed to Charles I's reign. A country interpretation of this work, dating from around the end of the century, consisted of light and dark geometrical inlay, such as the eight-pointed star in bone and ebony. This may be associated with the Tunbridge woodwork developed as a "souvenir" trade for visitors to the famous springs.

The Restoration marked the real development of English walnut furniture, however—with beech, then French walnut and, still later, "black" Virginia walnut supplementing the native wood. At first it was treated in the solid, like oak, but with more delicate carving. It proved wasteful when used in large planks of heart-wood, however, and lacked the life and light that could be displayed in veneers cut at angles unusable in solid construction. Noblemen returning from exile at the Restoration were quick to demand the finer Continental treatment of the wood, and our craftsmen had perforce to learn the entirely new technique of veneer. This meant as great a revision of their ideas as the medieval change to panel construction.

The technique of veneer consisted in covering a basic carcase of cheaper wood with thin layers of finely figured walnut—hand-sawn, six or seven to the inch in the seventeenth and eighteenth centuries. Glue was applied to affix the veneers, and when a strongly curved surface was covered a "caul" was first used to mould the veneer under heat. Cornice mouldings could thus be covered in cross-grained veneer; but English workmen only gradually learnt such practices and never accepted all the Continental methods. Edges might be protected with narrow beading.

To the furniture maker all this meant discarding the excellent oak technique. Veneers required smooth, flat surfaces instead of panels. The framing had to be secured by dovetailing and adhesive—often home-made "cheese glue" of milk curds: manufactured glue dated from about 1710 and was not patented until 1754, and bone glue fifty years later. Even the common dovetail (Fig. 16A) on such details as drawer fronts presented too much end-grain for satisfactory veneering and the lap dovetail (Fig. 16B) was substituted by about 1695. Dutch work of the eighteenth century may often be distinguished by continued use of the older "through" dovetailing.

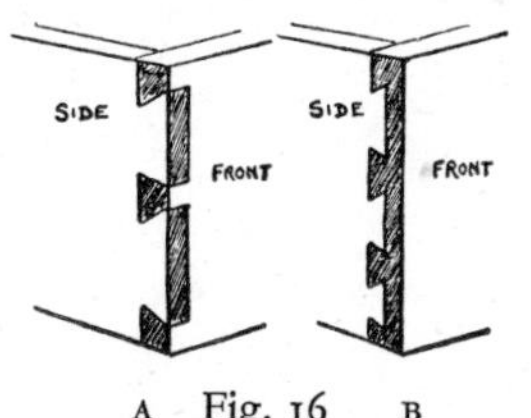

A Fig. 16 B

Oak, reacting strongly to atmospheric changes, was unsatisfactory as the carcase wood and was used chiefly for such features as drawer linings to take the rub of use. In the 1690's yellow deal (probably Norwegian spruce or silver fir) became popular as the basis. The veneers themselves were named for their patterns: although dominated by walnut they included many other woods—yew, for example, being used extensively for high quality veneers, although as a solid wood it was principally found in country furniture. The "crotch" veneer with its plume effect was obtained from the tree where a side branch grew away from the main trunk; the "whorl" or "oyster" being sliced transversely from a branch or small tree-trunk to show the annual growth rings around the heart (laburnum wood and dark, greenish olive were also much used for oyster veneer). The "burr", most difficult to lay because composed of fragile fibres and varying grains, was obtained from malformations caused by chance injuries to the tree and from the tree stump where the roots began showing infinitesimal veins suggestive of tousled, unwashed wool with the burrs still clinging to it. In high quality work the brilliance of these veneers was enhanced by repeated varnishing with gum lac dissolved in spirits of wine.

Other constructional innovations were the use of split caning on the backs of chairs, the introduction of screws—unpointed and finished with hand filing—and the greater use of glue instead of dowel pins in mortise-and-tenon joints. Forms now became infinitely more varied: the important Flemish scroll (Fig. 17) in its numerous elaborations dated especially to the years 1675-90.

Fig. 17

By the reign of William and Mary yet another influx of foreign workers had resulted from the revocation of the Edict of Nantes (1685), the refugee French Protestants mingling with the strongly Spanish-influenced Dutch craftsmen who accompanied William. By the end of the century there was a notable rise in the general standards of comfort. Houses were now being built with taller rooms, their panelling featuring strongly projecting dado and skirting with the tall upper panels topped by classic cornices. Even by Anne's reign these features contributed notably to furniture fashions in which the new emphasis was on height; particularly tall and narrow furniture was devised to fit the piers of wall between the two or three tall sash windows that graced the fashionable stateroom. Queen Mary created a vogue for porcelain and delft-ware collection, and therefore for china cabinets in which to display it. She also developed the French rage for needlework. Gorgeous silks were produced by the refugee Huguenot weavers, said to number eighty thousand, and the turn of the century was marked by much ornate upholstery, typified by the voluminously draped beds.

Pieces of furniture developed around the turn of the century reflected a more leisurely, cultured way of life, and included many card tables, bureaux and cabinets of every kind and, by the end of Anne's reign, the tallboy and a wealth of furniture for the previously ill-equipped bedroom. Materials included walnut in solid and veneer; oak for country work; finer caning for chair and day-bed; gesso, lacquer, and japanning, which may better be regarded as decorative media. Form showed great emphasis on tall, heavily pedimented furniture, lower articles such as chests of drawers often being raised on stands. Among other constructional details, perhaps the most typical leg of the late seventeenth century was the design with a "Spanish" bulb, mushroom, or inverted cup knee, round or many sided, tapering to a slim ankle above a less swelling foot. Sometimes the knee was made separately to minimize wastage of the expensive wood. But soon the turn of the century was witnessing an entirely new emphasis on curves, typified by the arched cornices of cabinet work, the series of curves that composed the chair-back, and most especially the cabriole leg.

Fig. 18

Regarding mounts, many Restoration handles were hollow pear or acorn shapes on circular plates, held by strips of metal which folded outwards inside the piece of furniture on the brass paper-clip principle, and were of brass instead of iron (Fig. 18). Others were wide low loops on irregularly shaped backplates (Fig. 19), sometimes lightly incised but not pierced until the 1720's. The early loop was hung on wires but after the turn of the century a good quality example would hang from the heads of the nutted bolts that held the back-plate (Fig. 20).

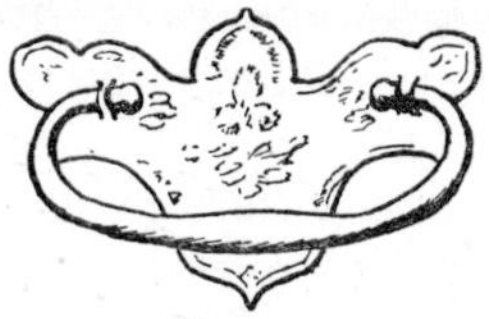

Fig. 19

Decoration was immensely important in the walnut period and included much gilded and silvered wood, but the most conspicuous feature was the marquetry work. Into grounds of straight-grain or oyster wood veneer, patterns cut from other, usually lighter, woods were fitted and glued with consummate skill. Sometimes the walnut was bleached, sometimes dyed black—now faded brown—to increase the colour contrasts. It must be emphasized that marquetry was carried out entirely in veneers, resembling the fitting of a jigsaw puzzle, as contrasted with inlay in which the pattern was inserted in a prepared ground of the solid wood. Woods in use at this period included chestnut, holly, laburnum, fruitwoods, yew, box, pine, sycamore, and lignum vitæ.

Fig. 20

Early work, before 1690, was in the Dutch manner, consisting of isolated panels showing naturalistic foliage and birds, with jasmine flowers, roses, and carnations depicted in ivory, bone, and mother-of-pearl as well as scorched and green-dyed holly and other colourful woods. But the colour was soon toned down to browns, buffs, and black with acanthus leaves and long-tailed birds preparing the way for still more formal scrolling. By 1700 flowers and then birds had disappeared, the dominant "core" of pattern featured in the Moorish type of arabesques soon becoming lost in spiky scrolls closely interwoven—the seaweed or endive style of the last phase, made only of box or holly wood on a walnut ground. This required extremely delicate cutting with a fine saw held at a slight angle.

By 1700 marquetry was becoming less popular and plain veneer more prevalent. The associated craft of parquetry consisted of a mosaic or "tesselation" of woods in simple geometrical forms entirely covering the prepared ground. Striped effects were achieved by slicing the veneer—laburnum was much used—longitudinally to include lines of sap wood and heart wood in each segment. Alternatively, contrasting woods might be used together.

The great walnut period is generally dated 1660-1730—better extended to about 1750—and is apt to overshadow that other important furniture treatment of these years, lacquer-work. Oriental lacquer was imported by the East India Company as early as Charles II's reign: the quantity can be judged by the fact that in 1750 three shiploads were sold for £200,000, including lacquer boards for making up in this country. But it was a very inferior home-produced and often amateur-decorated "japan" work that became particularly popular in post-Restoration England, the process being described in such works as the 1688 treatise by Stalker and Parker. It was a cheap substitute for the colourful veneers favoured on the Continent, and whole rooms were hung with lacquer boards. The demand for quality work had largely disappeared by 1730, but the practice was continued with varying enthusiasm throughout much of the eighteenth century: Horace Walpole in 1743 referred to "the modern japanning by ladies" and there was a brief revival in the mid-eighteenth century.

In quality work the English product was quite elaborately prepared, the carcase often veneered in smooth-grained wood. Raised designs were produced with a gesso-like base of whiting and size and, on a foundation of black, red, blue or more rarely green or yellow, the decoration was applied in gold, silver, and colour. Nearly all the designs were more or less eastern and the opaque paints were mixed with hard lacquer varnishes, though all lacked the genuine sap of the gum tree *rhus vernicifera* used in Oriental work. The mid-century produced various cheaper and altogether inferior methods, until the term japanning was applied to what was merely varnished oil painting. There was a nineteenth century vogue for furniture of japanned papier mâché.

Italian-styled gilded gesso was another, lesser vogue. This came in between 1695 and 1700 and remained popular for some forty years among a wealthy minority. Designs in light relief were moulded—the finest built up in delicate brush work—in a composition of whiting and size upon a base of pine; high relief details were carved in wood, glued in position and then coated with the same material. Outlines might be sharpened with hand tools before the whole was richly gilded or silvered.

The gilding of furniture was itself a laborious process, water-gilding being used for all good quality work. R.W. Symonds has pointed out that the final coats of size under the burnished areas of gold leaf varied in colour from period to period—brown during the William-Anne years, reddish-brown during those of George I and George II, brighter red in the so-called Chippendale period, and old rose or mauve-pink in the Adam period and late eighteenth century. For cheapness some work was covered with silver and then coloured gold. Collectors value only original mellowed gilding, quite different from the "dead" appearance of the cheaper oil gilding in which the leaf was cemented with fat oil instead of size.

The *early Georgian period* covered the reigns of George I (1714-27) and George II (1727-60), but these Hanoverian monarchs themselves contributed nothing to English furniture development in this particularly restless, creative century. By now there was a marked cleavage between the purely functional furniture of the poorer home and that introduced for its decorative value by the rich. In place of the individual specialist craftsman-retailer, master-craftsmen were now becoming established who could employ workers in a range of trades covering all kinds of furniture and could so supply non-manufacturing retailers.

The early part of the period showed rather heavy-handed

versions of Queen Anne furniture. There were many weighty pediments (Fig. 21), including the "broken" lines, curved, angular, and still clumsier "swan-neck", and the graceful cabriole leg became more heavily and realistically carved on the knee and based on a sturdy ball-and-claw (or lion's paw) foot (Fig. 22). But there was a noticeable increase in the preliminary consideration of furniture design among makers. At its most extreme, among a rich minority, furniture was handled as an architectural feature. Such leaders as William Kent (1684-1748) designed heavy Italianesque architectural furniture to suit the Palladian style of the mansions they devised in response to the Italian mood among the well-travelled élite. These houses had immensely tall and spacious staterooms with massive chimney pieces, richly moulded doorways, and, frequently, painted stucco walls instead of panelling. Gilding and gesso work, rich brass mounts, finely constructed chairs in the early Spanish mahogany, and prodigious elaborations of carving suited such a setting, and the bookcase and cabinet furniture was particularly notable.

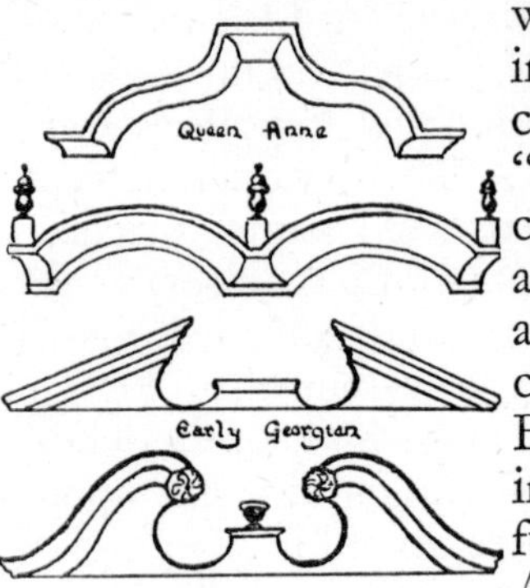

Fig. 21

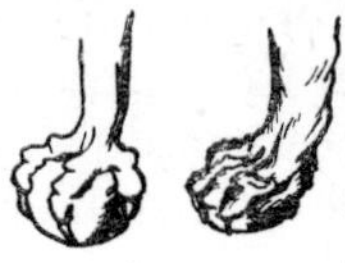

Fig. 22

For country pieces the main material was still oak, and for much quality work, especially in the bedroom, it was walnut. But the vogue for walnut was nearly over. The severe winter of 1709 had killed most of the walnut trees in Central Europe, this timber being quickly "cornered" by the Dutch. By 1720 the French found it necessary to put an embargo on the export of their home-grown walnut. Good quality English walnut had always been scarce, beech serving as a cheap but poor substitute, much affected by worm, and when Continental supplies ceased only the "black" Virginian variety was available.

Meantime, the arrival of a galleon loaded with mahogany had been mentioned in the *London Gazette* during 1703. This wood had been imported spasmodically during the seventeenth century, but the import duty on such exotic woods, calculated by weight, was so great that only the finest quality was used, for ultra-expensive work. Only when the tax was removed in 1733 did solid construction in a foreign wood become a practical proposition. This early mahogany was mainly "Spanish" from Santo Domingo, where apparently it was used by some of the earliest Spanish colonists around 1510. It was immensely strong, tough wood in trunks of huge girth—ideal for such purposes as table tops. As demand increased, Cuban wood, better figured and not liable to darken with exposure, was introduced, and in 1753 more than 500,000 cubic feet were imported from Jamaica. But while the beauty of the wood in veneer, such as the Cuban "curl", was only developed fully in the second half of the century, the early Georgian carver at once seized upon the wood in the solid as an ideal medium for his fiercely naturalistic work.

Fig. 23

Such carved motifs as eagles' heads and escallop shells (Fig. 23) were most popular during the period 1714-25; lions' heads during the period 1720-35; and satyrs' heads, 1730-40. There was naturally much overlapping, however, and a piece of furniture might have lion's paw feet associated with satyr's head and classic honeysuckle motifs carved on the knees of its cabriole legs. The cabochon-and-leaf motif (Fig. 24 shows two typical examples)—the French representation of a polished jewel—appeared from about 1735 onwards and was used by Thomas Chippendale in his early work. It is indicative of the increasingly French trend in furniture from the 1740's that trade catalogues began to apply the word *commode* to every kind of decorative furniture with drawers—a natural reaction from so much Dutch influence.

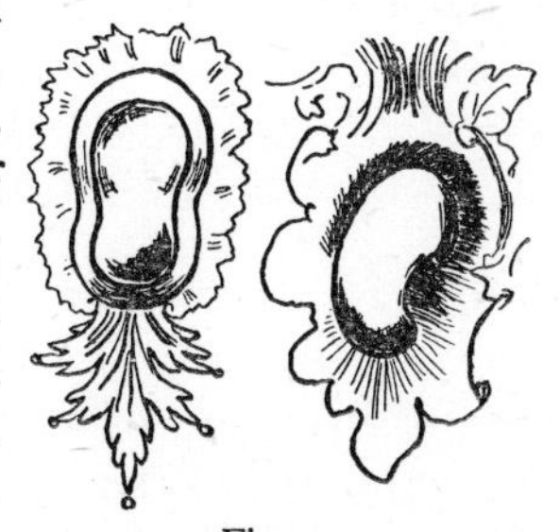

Fig. 24

It was this taste for lighter, daintier furniture that was caught by Thomas Chippendale (1718-79), most famous member of the Chippendale family, whose name must be associated with a period rather than with any individual products of his hand. Like other personalities of the eighteenth century such as Hepplewhite and Sheraton, he published designs for furniture which reflected and emphasized rather than created styles, and for which his employee Mathias Lock must receive much of the credit. He took the heavy furniture that had come in with Queen Anne and gave, for example, the cabriole leg a new lightness and rhythm with his French knurl (Fig. 25) and scroll (Fig. 26) toes. Cornices became smaller, lighter, often decorated with a dentil course (Fig. 27). Chippendale continued to favour the changing French fashions throughout his life, and became pre-eminent as an exponent of the classical style of the 1770's. Some of the later rococo work linked with his name—and generally executed by others—tended to go to extremes. Ince and Mayhew (approximately 1762), Edwards and Darly in 1754 and Thomas Johnson in 1758 were typical in their designs for this ultra-rococo and "Chinese" ornament.

Fig. 25

Fig. 26

Much rococo design showed an intermingling of the so-called "Chinese" and less extensive "Gothic revival" styles of the mid-century seen in furniture, silver, plaster, and stone work. Early in the eighteenth century a distinctively Chinese flavour was already to be found in many European fashions, including the ultra-rococo work of the French Meissonier and Jacques Caffieri. As early as 1685 William Temple in *Garden of Epicurus* had praised such Chinese techniques as lacquering, and from garden pavilions and exotic wallpapers (Evelyn refers to Chinese hangings in Queen Mary's Oriental apartments in 1693) the craze came to be applied, around the mid-eighteenth century, to many pieces of household furniture. Sir William Chambers, the first architect to visit China, was associated with the craze, although in 1757 he was stressing that the fashion was "unfit for our climate" and "much inferior to the antique".

Fig. 27

As to the Gothic travesty of medieval art supported by Horace Walpole, as early as 1711 Addison, in his literary sphere, was deploring a "Gothic Taste which has taken possession of us". In furniture the fancy for Gothic window tracery and arch and pillar forms was just a second mid-century diversion that can easily be taken too seriously: at the time furniture makers appear to have accepted and mingled French, Chinese, and Gothic motifs with light-hearted inconsequence. In general, only the ornament was affected, form remaining largely contemporary—an important distinction when comparing it with nineteenth century trends.

This was a great period for books of furniture design—more or less illustrated trade lists. One of the earliest was published in 1739 by the architect William Jones and included some "architect's furniture". But the most famous was Chippendale's *The Gentleman and Cabinet-Maker's Director* (1754, 1755, 1762). Its first edition circulated to over 300 subscribers of whom 140 were cabinet-makers and the like up and down the country.

Fig. 28

Construction at this time showed much use of architectural, pedimented furniture. Chippendale favoured cornices surmounted by fret-cut cresting (Fig. 28), expressive of his consummate skill in handling mahogany. Cabriole legs were still prevalent but some "Chinese" furniture returned to straight, untapering legs with stretchers. Early handles were drop loops on shaped backplates, solid or pierced. In the late 1730's stouter drop loops developed, each bolt head mounted on a separate moulded circle (Fig. 29). Elaborate French mounts came in around the mid-century (Fig. 30). Decoration included the increasing use of carving already described, with japanning for cheap work. Fret-cut and card-cut wood-

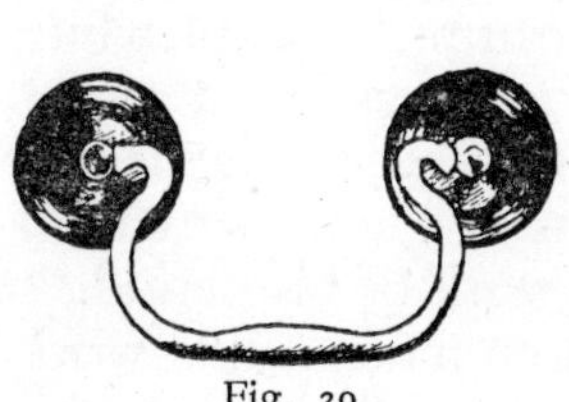

Fig. 29

Fig. 30

work was a feature of much "Chinese" furniture. The finest quality was carved out of the solid wood; the rest fret-sawn by hand and glued on—less regular than the modern machine product. Cheap "Chinese" furniture was often painted in plain colours with touches of contrasting shades in the frets.

The *George III period*, covering the years 1760-1810 and the Regency period 1810-20, was dominated by another great "name", the architect and furniture designer (not maker), courtier, and Member of Parliament, Robert Adam, foremost of four brothers, for whom both Chippendale and Hepplewhite executed a considerable amount of work. Adam's influence dated from 1758 when he returned from a tour of Italy and Dalmatia to dispel the Chinese and Gothic fantasies with a restrained classic style which he described as "the beautiful spirit of antiquity". This reflected much contemporary French feeling, in the Louis XVI style, as contrasted with the Louis XV style followed in Chippendale's *Director*, showing the same appreciation of the Pompeii and Herculaneum discoveries of earlier in the century. Adam is particularly valued today for his insistence that furniture and fittings should conform in every way to their architectural surroundings and like Kent he made himself responsible for all details in the houses he designed.

Adam died in 1792. In comparison, his contemporary, George Hepplewhite (died 1786; his *Cabinet Maker and Upholsterer's Guide* was published by the firm, A. Hepplewhite and Company, in 1788, 1789, and 1794) was but a minor contributor to furniture fashions. He specifically denied originality for his ideas but reflected with a homelier charm much that was most gracious in the work of his period.

Another important designer to whom much actual work is wrongly attributed was Thomas Sheraton (born 1751 and working in London between 1790 and his death in 1806). In his most famous publications *The Cabinet Maker and Upholsterer's Drawing Book*, 1791-94, which had nearly 650 subscribers, and *The Cabinet Dictionary*, 1803, he set on record his own and contemporary designs for furniture which contributed grace if not robustness to much work of the period. Basing his work on geometrical principles, he generally refused to tolerate ornament for its own sake, but towards the end of a life dogged by extreme poverty he tried to catch public approval with designs unworthy of his skill and versatility.

Articles of furniture particularly associated with this period included the sideboard and a multitude of little tables for drawing room decoration and for the fashionable bedroom breakfast, of which the most notable were the tripod and Pembroke varieties. Materials included great quantities of mahogany. The Honduras mahogany imported from Central America under the name of baywood during the second half of the century was of even grain, with few knots, little given to warping and easier to work than the Spanish variety. This was a fine basis for veneer, but it must be understood that much of the mahogany veneer of this period was mounted on red pine. The lovely Cuban mahogany veneers date from about 1770. And at the same time the baywood was misapplied as a veneer over cheap woods to simulate solid mahogany. It was usually stained and, being comparatively soft, was often treated with a wash of gum lac in spirit before being repeatedly waxed; much other eighteenth century woodwork was left entirely untreated and was cleaned with soap, water and sand.

For high quality work, however, the later eighteenth century chose such varied woods as satin-wood, popular in both solid and veneer between 1770 and 1795, harewood (stained sycamore), tulip, rosewood and kingwood. Forms were distinctively classic, elegantly proportioned, the legs finely tapering, usually in square section (thermed) at first but later often turned and fluted. A feature of the glazed cabinet work after about 1765 was the use of cross-grain veneer borders, mitred at the corners. But, in contrast to earlier walnut practice, veneered mouldings continued to be run with the grain. Carved mouldings lost favour in the last quarter of the century. There was much play with serpentine and bow outlines, and chair-backs were particularly varied. Handles lost their rococo extravagance in favour of elliptical and circular backplates (Fig. 31), the

Fig. 31

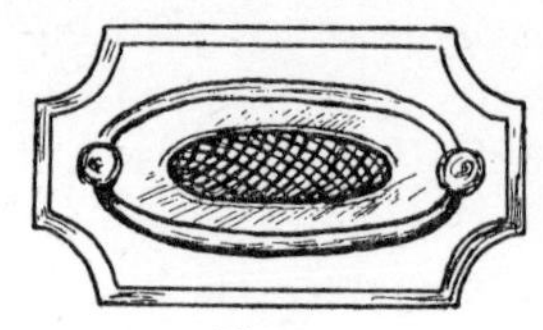
Fig. 32

loops and ring handles following the same outlines; in the late 1770's cast plates began to lose favour when a Birmingham firm devised a simple stamping method to produce patterns in relief (Fig. 32).

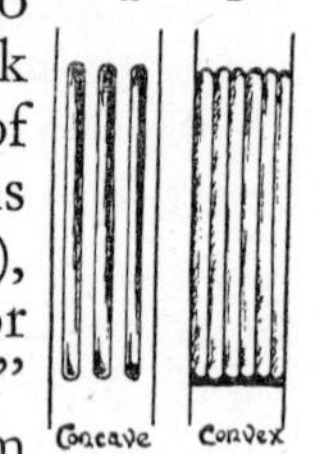

Fig. 33

Decoration on frieze, legs, and so on included much fluted and reeded work (Fig. 33, A and B) and carving in low relief of such classical motifs as pateræ (Fig. 34), urns and vases, swags (Fig. 35), husks (Fig. 36), and Adam's favourite motif, the anthemium or honeysuckle (Fig. 37). The "pear-drop" cornice bed-mould (Fig. 38) dated from about 1770. In preference to carving, Adam revived a fashion for colour—gilding, graceful panels of marquetry, inlay, marble and composition imitations and most especially paintings in the style of such imported decorators as Pergolesi and Angelica Kauffmann—the same decorations often appearing on ceilings, carpets and furniture.

Fig. 34

Adam greatly favoured the introduction of these round or elliptical plaques painted with cupids, classical figures or pastoral scenes. Some artists, such as Pergolesi, intended their decoration to be painted over a surface entirely covered with white enamel, under which any indigenous wood might be used, but in other pieces the glow of satinwood served as a brilliant background. Such Italian-inspired work was distinct from the cheaper style of painting found contemporaneously. Both were of western as opposed to Oriental inspiration, but while Adam and his Italian workers surrounded their central plaques with painted vases, swags, honeysuckle, and similar classical architectural motifs, others imitated the French school of work in the

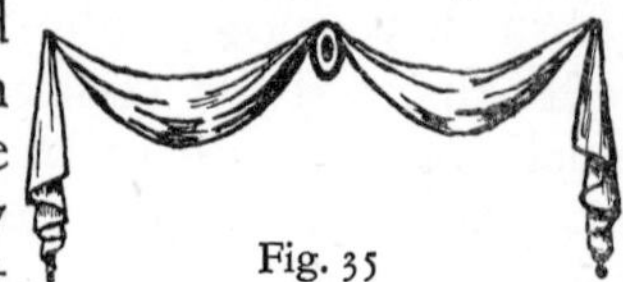
Fig. 35

Fig. 36

Vernis-Martin varnish, dominated by floral and foliage motifs—wreaths of roses, festoons, twisted ribbons, and so on.

Painted furniture was probably at its best between 1770 and 1780, but was excessively used nearer the end of the century and after. Sheraton recognized the danger of too much detail in this work and warned against "niggling and meanness"; but there was much amateur work: Jane Austen's Mr. Bingley declared that "all young ladies are accomplished and all paint tables, cover screens and net purses".

Fig. 37

Even by 1800 there was an appreciable deterioration in furniture styles. *Regency* work (too narrowly dated 1810-20) reflected the various Directoire (1795) and Empire (1804) styles in France, the classicism that caught France and then England being expressed in rather misguided strivings to reproduce the actual furniture of ancient Rome, Greece, and Egypt, in an archæological spirit, followed in France by a renewal of the rococo. The erudite Thomas Hope in his *Household Furniture and Decoration* (1807) stressed the chastity and play of contour, the breadth and repose of surface, and the opposition of plain and enriched parts, but he stressed, too, that Egyptian symbolism, for example, was unsuited to the average house.

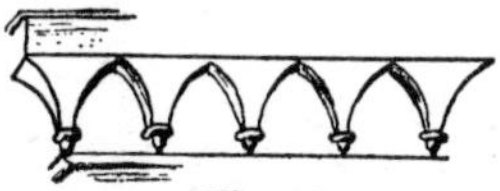

Fig. 38

Form and construction were massive, often over-elaborate. Materials included shining veneers of many striking, exotic woods, and rosewood was in particular demand. Ancient Roman marble slabs on lion-head supports prompted the more extensive use of marble and the composition scagliola, in and out of fashion throughout much of the eighteenth century. There was extensive application of bronzing and gilding and of the metal inlay which Robert Clayton's method (patented in 1818) reduced to great simplicity, any non-tarnishing metal, fusible at low temperature, being poured into incisions cut or punched in the wood. Handles, from about 1790, included many cast raised lion heads, some holding rings in their mouths.

By 1833 J. C. Loudon was able to define the principal styles of furniture design as the most prevalent "Grecian or modern", the Gothic or perpendicular, the Elizabethan combination of Gothic and Italian, and the florid Italian of the Louis XIV age. Already the fine discrimination of the previous century was gone. Indeed, even by the first decade of the new century a few, such as Thomas Hope, foresaw that the greatest safeguard against ungainly extravagance, an inborn sense of pride in honest design and workmanship, was soon to suffer in competition with machine productions. Yet in 1808 in his *Household Furniture* George Smith could declare in all seriousness, regarding "ornament and domestic embellishment", that "perfection it appears was reserved for the present period".

2

CHESTS

THE chest or coffer was among man's first crude efforts to make his dwelling a home. For centuries, in England, it was his trunk, his treasury, his store for arms, grain, clothing and linen. At a time when it was customary to sleep, eat, and work among skins and rushes heaped on the damp earth floor, the chest offered comparative comfort as seat and bed. It is given literary mention as early as A.D. 700. When the feudal lords of later centuries travelled from castle to castle, horse-borne chests or "trussing coffers" transported their furniture and belongings. Even in Tudor England chairs were so scarce that chest and stool were the usual seats. Yet by Georgian days the chest had all but disappeared, little beyond the name remaining in its direct descendant, the post-Restoration chest of drawers.

The names chest and coffer are generally used indiscriminately, but in 1662 Randle Holme made the distinction that a coffer "if it haue a streight, and flat couer, is called a chest, which in all other things represents the coffer, saue the want of a circular lid or couer".

The rounded cover was a natural relic of the earliest pre-Conquest type of chest or "dug-out". This was no more than a length of tree trunk roughly squared up, with the "lid" split off longitudinally and the box hollowed out with an adze and bound with iron. From this developed crude plank chests such as Henry II ordered should be placed in all churches for contributions to the relief of the Holy Land. By the thirteenth century the making of plank chests had become a sufficiently important craft for a Guild of Cofferers to be established. The quality of that simple early workmanship may be judged by the fact that more than a hundred chests made before 1400 are still preserved in churches and museums.

These massive pieces were made of oak planks split with a rivening tool in the manner described in the previous chapter. "Borded chests" built from these early planks were of the simplest, most obvious construction which, for that very reason, remained in common use for some three hundred years. As late as the seventeenth century some chests were still being made with sides and base of planks crudely attached to upright end-boards by wooden dowel pins, hand-wrought nails or bands of iron, and decorated with gouge-cut edges. But by then they were smaller, lighter affairs, of planks less than an inch thick, with dovetailing to unite the plank ends in a workmanlike joint.

The other principal medieval style had front and back each formed of three or more planks, two as uprights supporting a central one laid horizontally. The uprights or "stiles" often raised the chest well above the trampled rushes of the primitive floor; other chests were legless and fastened to the ground for safety. Alternatively, during the fifteenth century, the leg might be formed by the equally simple lengthening of the board at each end of the chest, which was grooved to support the sides and was frequently shaped to give the appearance of two feet.

The early lid, which was often canted, opened on a pin hinge revolving on a horizontal pivot socketed into the uprights, a method which continued until the fifteenth century, although largely replaced after the thirteenth century by the strap hinge. Iron hinges were used in association with iron bandings. Coffers designed for being roped on to horses had rounded lids and large, squarish handles on the ends. Often they were strengthened with iron scrollwork applied over leather—a smoother field than the rough wood for the painting and gilding beloved of the Middle Ages—or over cloth, including rich Genoa velvet embroidered with the owner's arms or initials.

Early in the fourteenth century, however, the wood itself was being worked smooth enough to encourage attempts at carved decoration. At first these efforts principally consisted of Gothic circles and similar formal work, but as the century progressed chests made for the nobility might show fabulous monsters, armorial shields and other ambitious efforts. On the "tilting chests" associated with the fifteenth century, jousts and deeds of arms and especially the triumph of St. George over the dragon were elaborately and realistically portrayed.

Colour, however, continued to be the most important decorative medium until the middle of the sixteenth century. Chests still exist showing colourful tempera decoration inside the lid although centuries of wear have removed this enrichment from the outside carving.

External locks were important decorative features of all these chests, whether for church or for home use. A finely wrought hinged staple was attached to the lid so that when this was closed the staple fitted into the lock through a hole in the face-plate. Chains at the back were another precaution and the hinge itself might consist of two iron staples linked together.

By far the most notable advance in chest construction was the development of the framed-up, panelled coffer, of which specimens dating from earlier than the late sixteenth century are now rare. This new frame chest, its construction described in Chapter 1, again exemplified the old woodworker's appreciation of his particularly difficult wood which was still most usually oak, the panels being held without fixing in the grooved stiles, rails, and muntins which formed the chest framework. When it was fitted with an inner compartment this, too, was merely held in grooves.

The lid might be formed of two or three boards, or, more especially in north country work, panelled like the front. Transverse cross bearers on the under side held the boarded lid together, showing outside the chest when the lid was closed.

Framed chests offered great scope for carving which, by the fifteenth century, was becoming fairly common, although considerably under the influence of work imported from Flanders. Towards the end of the fifteenth century several styles of single and double linen-fold panelling came into vogue: after about 1530 these tended to greater elaboration, but English craftsmen eschewed the ornate Continental work of the fifteenth and sixteenth centuries.

An innovation in Henry VIII's time (1509-47) was the cypress chest as a protection against moth, decorated in low relief. The cedar-wood chest for blankets and clothing came later, being largely imported from Holland in Queen Anne's reign. Fir from the Baltic countries was much used, too, in the fifteenth and sixteenth centuries, so that the chest was often referred to as the "spruce". Indeed, the chest, still being Jack-of-all-trades, had many names. Travelling chests were "standards". Chests with their lids scored for reckoning were more accurately "counters" than the shop furniture of today. Small coffers or coffrets were also "fosselletts" and were popular receptacles for documents, linen, and spices.

Although oak was still the staple wood of the English joiner, chestnut and elm chests were made. As walnut is subject to worm attack it is difficult to tell how much was used before the great walnut vogue that followed the Restoration.

Elizabethan coffers were often extremely large. Decoration varied from rich, coarse carving to simple mouldings on the framing. The back was seldom carved but at the front arcaded panels, typifying what is known as the Renaissance style, might be divided by richly carved pilasters (Fig. 39) and among the wealth of decorative motifs space might be reserved for the owner's initials or for the year of marriage in the case of the bride's dower chest—an utterly essential article, as the portable cupboard was as yet a rarity.

Fig. 39

As the sixteenth century progressed the carving on the stiles sometimes took the form of the profile caryatid popular on contemporary firedogs. Even in country work Continental ideas were having their effect on the old Gothic traditions. As chairs were still scarce, chests and stools were made in abundance during this century, but probably for this very reason carving began

A seventeenth-century country
›iner's interpretation of the
amed-up chest showing a crude
›mbination of chequer inlay,
ouge cuts, and glued-on
decoration.

b. Strapwork decoration in low relief around panels finely inlaid with flower-and-vase motifs are characteristic of the early seventeenth century. The corner stiles form the feet, overlapped by a base moulding.

Raised panels, pearl-inlaid and
ith their corners skilfully mitred,
ıte this oak mule chest to the
ter seventeenth century. The
ınels at the ends show the earlier
ıse chamfering used by the stone
mason.

a. With well-balanced corni and plinth, this chest drawers displays the mo extreme use of elaborate mitred corners, glued c bosses and split spindle The lower drawers are st enclosed within doors. Abo 1670.

b. The broad half-round veneered moulds around the drawers help to date this chest to the first years of the eighteenth century and its decoration illustrates the final phase in late Stuart marquetry work—the seaweed or endive design. The handles are not contemporary.

to lose some of its individuality. By 1600 mouldings tended to become thin and poor, and rails, stiles, and friezes lost much of their vigorous character.

Still with a feeling for colour, Italian-influenced craftsmen now inlaid light and dark woods in the light oak of some coffers. Detailed pictures of buildings were presented in this way on what are now known as Nonsuch chests and are generally assumed to represent the palace formerly at Ewell, Surrey. It has been suggested by Fred Roe, however, that the original of these exceptionally elaborate pieces may have been the somewhat later Nonesuch House on Old London Bridge. This enormous erection is said to have been made in Holland, early in Elizabeth's reign, and only assembled in this country.

James I's reign (1603-25) is generally known as a period of solid if unimaginative craftsmanship. Chests were now more usually panelled on all sides, the lids panelled and edged with thumb moulding (Fig. 40). But the carving on the front was restricted to little more than a variety of stock patterns—strips of repeat designs from which the required lengths were cut off without regard for the sequence of the outlines. Carving in abundance continued until 1650, the guilloche being a typically popular pattern. Projecting panels, glued-on bolection mouldings with elaborately mitred corners (Fig. 41) and split-turned decorations on the stiles and rails were employed around and after the mid-century. Chests inlaid with bone, ivory and shell have been dated to Charles I's reign, but were mostly post-Restoration products.

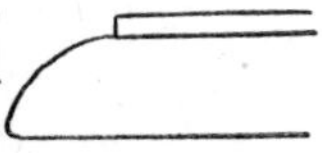

Fig. 40

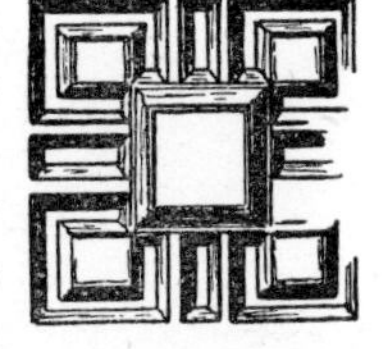

Fig. 41

By then, however, men were thinking of furniture very much more elaborate than the simple chest. Some of these late examples were raised on bun feet; even short cabriole legs followed in the next century. Some chests were placed upon stands of the type used beneath early chests of drawers. The lighter, gayer walnut was now gradually coming into fashion and occasional walnut "mule chests" are found—transitional pieces from which evolved the chest of drawers.

Oak chests, poorly carved, continued to be made into the eighteenth century and elaborate carving was a feature of such Georgian chests as were made of mahogany. Between 1680 and 1710 large blanket chests, some with domed lids, were often to be found in bedrooms, their decoration consisting of black and gold japanning in the popular Oriental manner. Rather later they were mounted on separate gilt stands.

It was the mule chest or drawer chest, the marriage cassone with its "bottom drawer", that marked the real break with traditional chest design. This first appeared in England in the sixteenth century with one wide drawer or two narrow ones tucked insignificantly beneath the deep coffer: in 1534 Catherine of Aragon had a coffer "having foure tilles therein, the fore fronte of every one of them gilte". By the end of the reign of William III the coffer had gone, entirely replaced by drawers. The chest had become the chest of drawers.

3

CHESTS OF DRAWERS

A FULL century passed before the transformation from chest to chest of drawers through the transitional mule chest could be regarded as complete. One early Stuart version consisted of a chest made in two separate parts, a sub-cornice marking the division at a little above half height. Above was a deep chest receptacle; below, three or four drawers of various depths were irregularly arranged behind panelled doors, an especially deep bottom drawer being provided for cavalier hats—a feature that continued until the end of the century.

The chief wood was still oak, occasionally walnut, with beech, elm, fruit woods, and pine for decorative applied mouldings and for the whole structure of much country work. Construction, therefore, was still in the old style which permitted the oak to react to atmospheric changes, uprights, rails, and muntins forming a grooved frame to hold the loose panels. Long side panels followed the lines of the doors, and when the doors were discarded these side panels were often sub-divided to match the horizontal lines of the drawer fronts. Mortise-and-tenon joints held the framework; coarse, simple, or "through" dovetailing joined front and sides of each drawer. Grooves sunk in the sides of the massive drawers fitted bearers which consisted of fillets of wood projecting from the sides of the chest itself. Large bun feet emphasized a general air of solidity.

The James I alliance with Spain may have given a fillip to the Moorish style of decoration in inlaid bone, ivory, and mother-of-pearl, but this was more typical of post-Restoration work, when high quality products, carried out entirely in oak, were showing the applied mouldings elaborately mitred and the split balusters and egg-shapes stained to resemble ebony seen on contemporary chests. Raised panels might be glued to heavily proportioned chests in which the lower drawers were still enclosed by doors.

Such furniture continued to be made for many years, but gradually after the restoration of the monarchy in 1660 the chest of drawers as known today became established, ousting the chest from the richer households where standards of comfort improved immeasurably before the end of the century. Samuel Pepys records buying for his bedroom "a fair chest of drawers" in the City in 1661.

Early examples of this late Stuart period were still frequently made of oak, although walnut was now becoming established, reflecting the Continental atmosphere of Charles II's court and his own encouragement of lavish building and decoration among the ladies who set its fashions. The construction showed drawers fitted with runners, their fronts decorated with moulded panels that lacked the shapings of earlier work. The substantial bun or ball feet (Fig. 42A) were gradually replaced by the bracket foot (Fig. 42B), and the old turned, carved, or shaped knobs on the drawers gave place, towards the end of the century, to brass escutcheons in elaborate designs and drawer pulls in acorn and pear shapes.

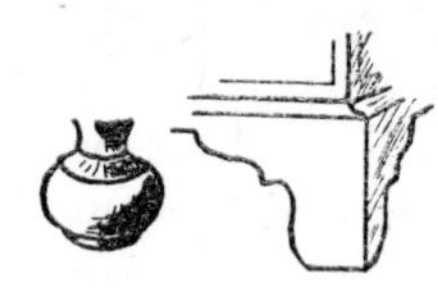

A Fig. 42 B

As early as Elizabethan days walnut had been highly regarded and walnut chests of drawers made before 1680 were still dominated by the traditional use of the solid wood. It took time for the Continental practices of veneer and marquetry to become established. Indeed, the second half of the seventeenth century showed many conflicting trends, for even the Dutch craftsmen accompanying William III were influenced by Italo-French and Spanish practices. Not until Anne's reign did styles become established with less French and more Dutch influence revealed in the more distinctively English designs.

By the reigns of William and Anne the typical chest of

drawers was a straight-fronted chest about forty inches high with five drawers. These were plain, but rounded bead moulding edged the framework around them. Large ovolo moulding was applied to the top edges of the chest around front and sides and was often matched by inverted moulding on the plinth above large bun, ball, or more often bracket feet, these last sometimes surrounding square blocks that carried the weight. On good chests of drawers even the sides were veneered, with straight grain or oyster pattern. Only such parts as the back showed the panel technique; elsewhere border inlay and bandings combined with the veneer to produce panel effects.

Marquetry-decorated chests of drawers dating from Charles II's reign were probably Dutch, but the fashion was well established in England early in the reign of William and Mary, native work being on flat, not curved, surfaces. These pieces were decorated on their tops, fronts, even their bracket feet. But throughout the period many others were plainly veneered in a variety of beautiful woods—yew, plane, pear, burr elm, tulip, and so on, ingeniously combined with walnut. Geometric lines in holly or box wood sometimes added to their dignity and in some instances herring-bone patterns were achieved with parquetry. Yet another form of decoration consisted of japanning in imitation of Oriental lacquer work.

Handles at this time were frequently drop-loops held to the backplates by brass or iron wire or, after about 1700, by the heads of the nutted bolts that attached the plates. Pierced designs dated from about 1720.

One result of Continental practice was a variation on the plainly solid type of chest of drawers, the chest being mounted on a separate stand consisting of a row of low arches. By the late 1680's the stand was being raised higher, on five or six stumpy turned or spiral twist legs joined by either turned or flat, waved stretchers. The stand then followed the trend of contemporary side tables. In the reign of William III it had one or two drawers in its framework, often mounted on tapering "peg-top" legs. The style continued into Queen Anne's reign (1702-14) made in walnut with S-shaped legs, narrower at first than the typical cabriole and sometimes terminating in the hoof foot. But the phase soon passed.

By 1710, as the chest-on-stand was beginning to lose favour, another variety of chest of drawers was developed, to become known as the tallboy. This consisted of two chests of drawers, one on top of the other. It was an architectural feature rather than a mere piece of furniture, with strongly-emphasized cornice in cross-grain veneer—sometimes hiding a secret drawer in the swell or pulvenated frieze, of convex profile as contrasted with the concave moulding known as the cavetto (Fig. 43). The balance of the cornice shaping, the slight reduction of width and depth in the upper chest and the frequent use of canted and fluted corners gave the tallboy a well-proportioned grace. The upper chest most often contained three long drawers and a top row of two or three small ones; the lower chest resembled the single chest of drawers already described except when cabriole legs were introduced, necessitating a reduction in the number of drawers. The splayed corners were veneered in cross-grain walnut, and veneered bands of herring-bone or feather-grain or the plainer cross-grain enhanced the drawer fronts, the popular herring-bone consisting of two rows of opposing diagonal grain.

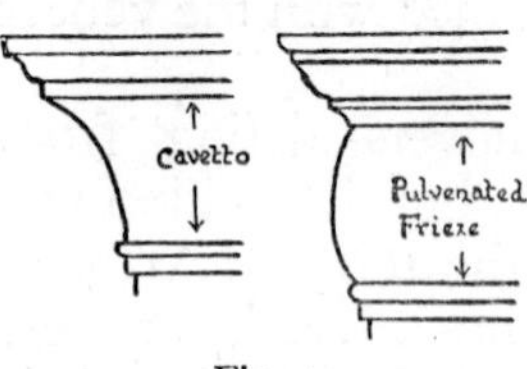

Fig. 43

Such bands of veneer, in conjunction with other features, are an aid in dating the chests of drawers of the period: from 1680 to 1705 there was a vogue for diagonal grain set at an angle of 45 degrees; cross-grain in combination with herring-bone was popular 1695-1715; after 1710, cross-grain veneer was often used alone. The corners of these bands were often square-butted, mitred corners indicating high quality work.

Mouldings applied round the drawer fronts are also a guide to approximate dates (Fig. 44 indicates typical outlines and profiles). During the period 1660-1705, half-round mouldings of solid walnut were often used (Fig. 44A), but by 1695 a twenty-year vogue was beginning for reeded mouldings, two or three together (Fig. 44B). Between about 1700 and 1725 the framing around the

\ transitional chest-on-stand, combining
en Anne and early Georgian features. The
vers show careful matching of their walnut
ers and have herringbone veneer borders,
bined with the early, heavy cock-bead
ng, and the open loop handles of the
's. The stand has legs and stretchers
nbling those of side tables of the 1700's.

b. An early-eighteenth-century walnut chest-on-stand, the stand showing apron shaping suggestive of contemporary dressing tables. Indications of high quality workmanship include the mitred corners to the veneered borders of the drawers, the beaded edging to the stand, protecting the veneer, and the cabriole shaping of back as well as front legs.

PLATE 5

Early-eighteenth-century tallboy with fluted chamfered corners with ogee stops. The drawers and writing slide are bordered with herringbone veneer and the central recess at the base is decorated with a sunray motif in the style of the period. About 1710.

drawer opening might be edged with a small bead (Fig. 44C) and from 1710 until 1735 a small lip moulding sometimes projected around each drawer itself—let into the solid of the drawer front so as to project from under the veneer (Fig. 44D). This was the forerunner of the popular applied cock-bead of the mahogany period, dating from 1730 (Fig. 44E), which projected outwards around the edge of the drawer front. After about 1715 the inside of the drawer had grooves in its sides to hold the bottom boards.

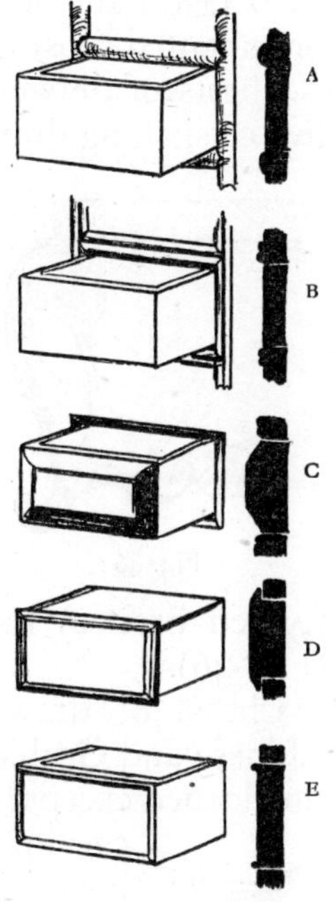

Fig. 44

The late years of the Queen Anne period produced great numbers of chests of drawers and tallboys, handsome, dignified, walnut pieces with simple veneers preferred to marquetry. But the popularity of walnut was gradually waning and before the middle of the century chests of drawers began to appear in the early Spanish mahogany. At first these were straight-fronted; the serpentine fronts associated with mahogany dated from the 1760's; bow fronts, although made earlier, were more particularly a feature of the last years of the century.

On the mahogany chest of drawers typical mid-century cornice moulding showed dentil and key patterns. Canted corners were usually fluted and carved or decorated with "Chinese" applied fret or lattice work, the carving of the period being very fine. The bracket feet often showed the cabriole profile (Fig. 45). Handles with pierced backplates continued in fashion, balanced by ornamental keyplates until about 1750 when sunk-flush escutcheons were often used. Stouter brass drop handles began to be used after about 1735, however, each bolt-head mounted on a separate pierced or engraved rose backplate. From

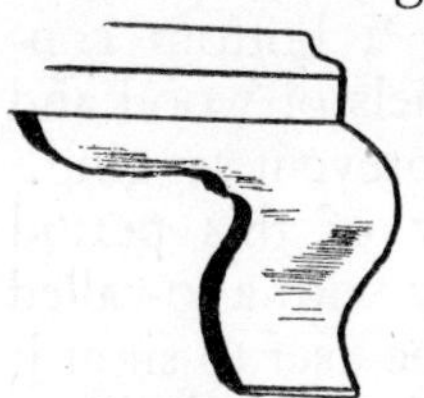
Fig. 45

1750 elaborate pulls and escutcheons in the French style ornamented those commodes that followed the French taste.

Chests of drawers were often tall enough, now, to carry five or six long drawers and two of half-width at the top, but many others from about 1750 were drawing-room commodes, low enough for the display of porcelain upon their highly polished tops. Chippendale gave much care to these pieces in the French style, with their serpentine fronts and sides, swelling *bombé* drawer profiles—or doors enclosing the drawers—graceful legs, rococo carving, and sometimes gilt ormolu (gilded bronze) mounts on front corners and front legs (Fig. 46).

Fig. 46

Chests of drawers escaped much of the mid-century Chinese and Gothic extravagance, for their fronts remained unadorned except for elaborate metal handles and keyplates, carving of top and plinth mouldings, mouldings between the drawers and, sometimes, shaped pilasters on the canted corners, perhaps fluted and topped with architectural capitals (Fig. 47). Japanning was particularly popular.

Drawers before 1750 might show the projecting lip moulding, but after 1745 the more usual finish was the applied half-round bead known as the cock-bead referred to above. Another detail regarding the drawers was the change, from about 1770, to a bottom constructed of two half-width panels of wood and fitted with a central bearer to prevent sagging.

Fig. 47

Many a chest of drawers and tallboy of this period followed the fashion of Queen Anne's day with a so-called brushing or writing slide which enabled the user to sit at it in comfort as a dressing table when a kneehole was lacking. The slide, framed in oak or mahogany, pulled out like a drawer with two minute brass drop-loops. But after 1765 there might be a hinge to the top drawer instead, so that the front opened flat, at the same time pulling out slightly (Fig. 48).

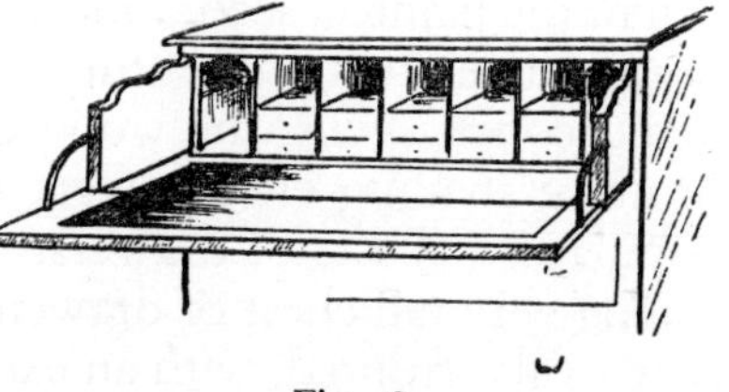
Fig. 48

Mahogany chests of drawers continued to be made into the nineteenth century, in both solid wood and veneer, but as the eighteenth century progressed popular taste turned to the lighter satinwood, sycamore, amboyna, zebrawood, stained woods, with a considerable amount of beech for cheap painted furniture. In keeping with the classicism of this period, chests of drawers after 1760 were frequently made with the plinth omitted and the vertical corner pieces carried uninterruptedly to the floor in an outward "French" curve. The bottom of the framing was then shaped to harmonize or the front of the bottom drawer extended downwards in shaped carving.

This is the period particularly associated with Hepplewhite's name in bedroom furniture. His early tallboy designs often showed moulded cornice, fluted frieze with pateræ (circular carved or turned discs) spaced between the flutings. He favoured fine brass drop handles and later circular embossed plates, harmonizing with his use of carved and inlaid circular rosettes and pateræ on drawers that nearly always were cock-beaded and veneered.

The new style of brass mount dated from about 1777 after which the backplates of the drawer pulls, circular, elliptical or octagonal, were ornamented with stamped relief work. Lion's head knobs, wreaths of flowers, cast heads holding rings and similar devices dated from about 1790. The turned mahogany knob, sometimes in a stamped brass surround, was produced from 1800.

The Sheraton style of chest of drawers is associated with the bow front; bow-fronted tallboys are rare, however, and Sheraton himself developed a great love of straight lines, rectangles, and square corners. Bracket feet were usual for tallboys; tapering reeded legs in many styles for commodes. Decoration often featured classic ornament and stringing, lines of inlay in ebony and satinwood or boxwood. By 1800 veneers of boldly figured foreign woods replaced to some extent the painted decoration of much cheap work produced in the late eighteenth century. Ovals containing beautifully inlaid conch shells, the wood often painted or scorched to produce shading effects, were a Sheraton period speciality popular on chests of drawers.

The very tall chest of drawers belongs to this late period, bow or flat fronted, with an exceptionally wide frieze above the top two drawers. Sometimes reeded quarter-columns were let into the front corners and turned feet continued the line.

Throughout this summary it has been possible only to indicate the leading fashions of the day. It must always be remembered that these greatly overlapped among country makers and great numbers of comparatively plain pieces were also produced, lacking the elaborations of the more expensive work. Oak chests of drawers continued to be made throughout the eighteenth century, plain but well constructed, but by the second half of the century craftsmanship was beginning to show the effects of cut-price competition. Veneer, for example, sometimes lost its original purpose, plain Honduras carcase wood being veneered on to pine chests of drawers to achieve the appearance of solid mahogany at a cheaper price.

A mahogany tallboy with fluted chamfered corners, cock-beaded drawers, and bracket feet, typical of many produced in the later eighteenth century. The top drawer of the lower section pulls out, the front hinged to fall flat for writing.

a. An example of the rich mahogany and excellent workmanship of about 1760. This serpentine dressing commode, with cluster-column pilasters and ornate mounts, has its top drawer elaborately fitted for toilet needs.

b. In cont the later y of the ei eenth cen sawcomm in satin-w and harewood, plain in outline but exquisitely decorated in contrasting woods urns, bows, and pendant husks.

4

CHAIRS OF THE OAK PERIOD

MORE than four thousand years ago chairs were being made with the mortise-and-tenon joints that were to dominate English oak furniture construction. In England, however, even by the end of the sixteenth century, chairs were still comparative rarities. E. W. Gregory, quoting the inventories of Gilling Castle, Yorks, shows that in 1594 the great chamber contained twenty-eight stools but only one chair, and, in 1624, thirty-five stools and two chairs. At the earlier date the dining parlour showed no chairs at all—merely buffet stools, forms, and cushions; even by 1624 only three chairs had been placed there. These were almost certainly armchairs, for the master of the house; the stools would be reserved for distinguished guests and the rest of the company would make do with movable forms and with benches fixed against the wall.

This is not to suggest that chairs were unknown to the country woodworker. M. Harris has shown that in 1478 chairs were among the pieces of everyday turnery work mentioned in documents relating to the Guild of Turners. But such comfort was still of little account in the English home.

In sixteenth-century England there appear to have been three main types of chair. Each was the product of a separate craft from which evolved, by the seventeenth century, that specialized, distinctive branch of joinery, the trade of chair-maker. The types of chair were the turner's "thrown" chair which obviously developed from the still simpler turned stool; the rare upholsterer's chair of classic origin (with joiner-made frame); the most important

Fig. 49. Thrown or turned chair back.
Fig. 50. Early form of X-chair.
Fig. 51. Early straight panels of box chair.
Fig. 52. Later oak with scrolling top and pronounced "ear-pieces".
Fig. 53. Mid-seventeenth-century "Yorkshire-Derbyshire" type.
Fig. 54. Charles II walnut.
Fig. 55. James II "periwig" type.
Fig. 56. William III, introduction of central splat.
Fig. 57. Anne-early Georgian.

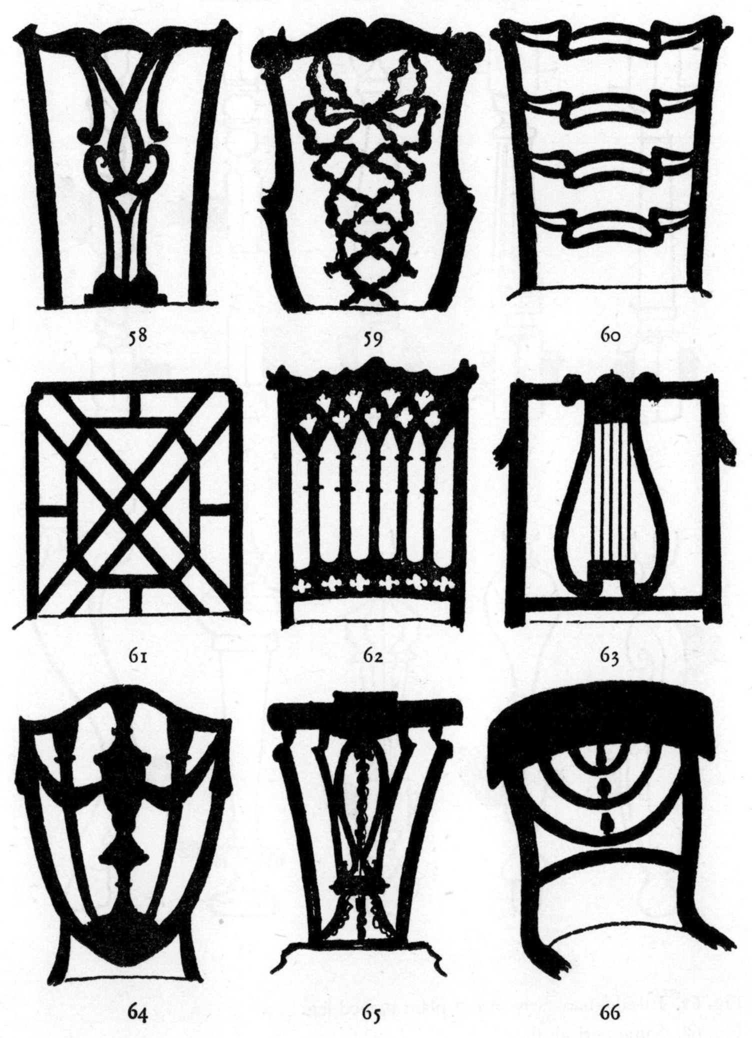

Fig. 58. Mid-eighteenth-century splat form.
Fig. 59. Typical ribband work, mid-eighteenth century.
Fig. 60. Ladder-back.
Fig. 61. "Chinese" trellis.
Fig. 62. "Gothic" tracery.
Fig. 63. "Lyre" design (Adam period).
Fig. 64. Shield with carved urn and drapery.
Fig. 65. "Straddling" chair as interpreted by Sheraton.
Fig. 66. Early-nineteenth-century shaping.

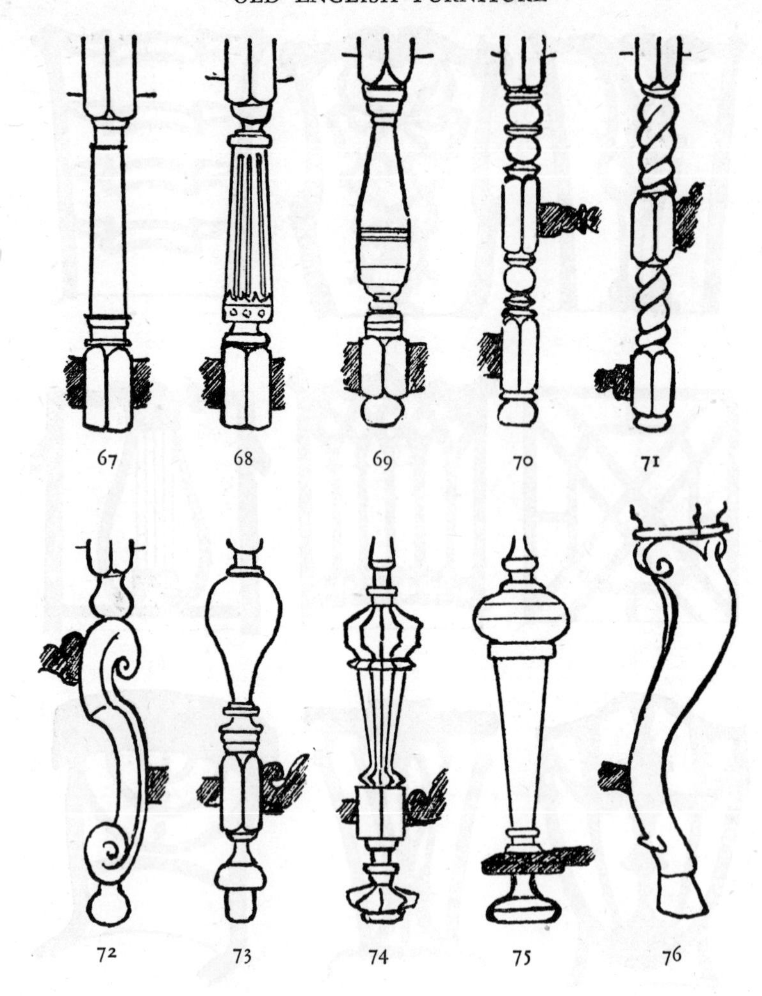

Fig. 67. Elizabethan-early Stuart plain turned leg.
Fig. 68. Same period, fluted.
Fig. 69. Early Stuart baluster turning.
Fig. 70. Mid-seventeenth-century bobbin-turned.
Fig. 71. Post-Restoration twist-turned.
Fig. 72. Post-Restoration S-curve.
Fig. 73. William III "Portuguese" swell.
Fig. 74. William III angular octagonal shaping.
Fig. 75. William III "mushroom" swell.
Fig. 76. Early cabriole, *c.*1700.

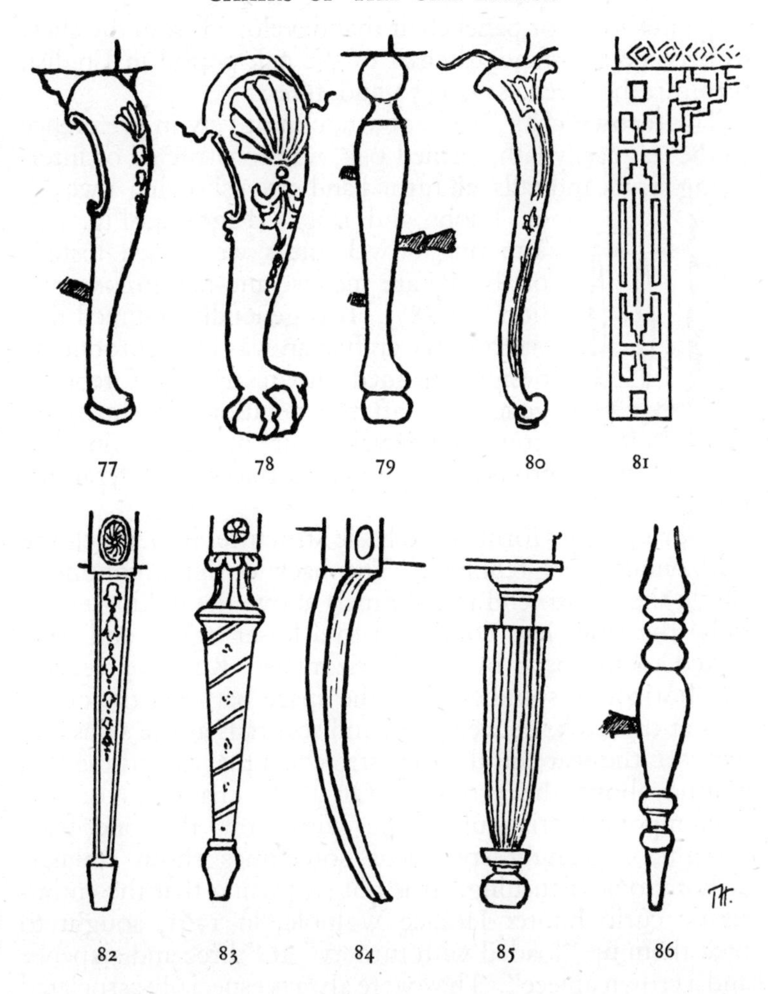

Fig. 77. Queen Anne cabriole.
Fig. 78. Early Georgian cabriole.
Fig. 79. Country adaptation of the cabriole.
Fig. 80. Mid-eighteenth-century "French" type.
Fig. 81. Fret-cut "Chinese".
Fig. 82. Square-section tapering (thermed), later eighteenth century.
Fig. 83. Round-section tapering, later eighteenth century.
Fig. 84. Tapering splay.
Fig. 85. Early-nineteenth-century leg.
Fig. 86. North country Windsor type, around 1800.

carpenter's box or panel chair that developed from the chest to become the standard chair of the oak period in English furniture between, say, 1550 and 1660.

The thrown chair, made of ash, elm or yew in preference to the less easily lathe-turned oak, was constructed of interlacing struts and rails, all turned and often showing a wealth of knobs and rings (Page 54, Fig. 49). Tapering dowel joints were used instead of the square mortise-and-tenon construction (Fig. 87). It is generally assumed that the country craftsman was but reproducing designs handed down by his forebears, generation after generation, of the traditional medieval chair illustrated in illuminated manuscripts and showing traces of Byzantine form.

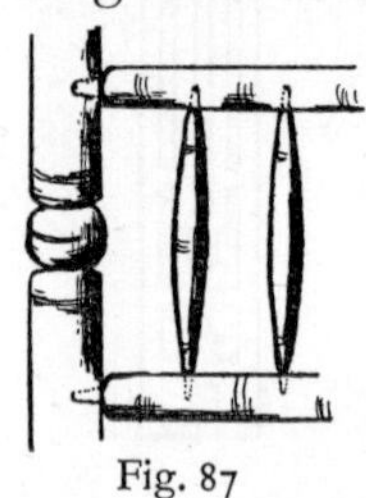
Fig. 87

Four uprights formed the basic structure, into which the horizontals were tenoned. The back uprights continued above the seat to end in tall finials above the linking cross-rails; the front legs continued to a lesser height and were linked to the back by arm horizontals. Rows of vertical and horizontal spindles filled the space between the cross-rails at the back, between arm and seat rails at the sides and between the seat and the four stretchers that linked the legs a little above the ground. On these chairs, as on the contemporary triangular type with only the one back upright, remaining specimens sometimes show fantastic elaborations of turning. It is not surprising that the enthusiastic curio hunter Horace Walpole, in 1761, sought to pick them up "loaded with turnery" at "three and sixpence and a crown apiece". They were always especially associated with Lancashire and Cheshire, the Welsh Marches, Herefordshire, and the West Country. In simple forms turned chairs continued to be made for a cheap market throughout succeeding centuries, and are described in Chapter 7.

In contrast, the classic X chair was an extravagant rarity, although Italian workmen employed by Henry VIII are supposed to have introduced it to this country. In the early sixteenth century it would appear to have been the prerogative of royalty, but during the seventeenth century must have been used in many a grand mansion. The legs, front and back, formed two rounded X shapes between which, on intersecting webbing, was slung a deeply-cushioned seat. The back consisted of fabric stretched between vertical continuations of the back X (Page 54, Fig. 50). The arms, running from the tops of the front X to the back uprights, were apparently shaped only in later examples, early ones being entirely straight and with the tops of the front X, like those of the back, finished with little pummels of metal. Later these were of cloth-covered wood, on the back uprights only. The entire chair was covered with some rich material such as velvet, held by brass-headed nails and edged with heavy fringes on arms and seat. Examples at Knole, Kent, among other plainer fabric-covered chairs, remain as noteworthy evidence of early upholstery and can be dated to about 1605.

Even among the well-to-do, however, most people throughout this period had still to make the best of an abundance of loose covers and cushions to mitigate the hardness of severely flat seat and uncurving back. Inventories of large houses of the early seventeenth century mention a wealth of needlework, crewel-work, and set-work, of velvet embroidered with cuts of cloth of gold and fringed with silk, of taffeta, sarcenet, figured satin, and most especially that woollen material, carpet-like, known as Turkey work. Tapestry weaving was given special encouragement in 1619 when James I established Flemish weavers at Mortlake.

A different form of X construction, of which sixteenth-century examples remain, but from churches rather than private houses, has been given the name of Glastonbury chair. In this the X was formed at each side of the chair by the crossing of front and back leg. Legs and seat members were flat rails, their junctions fastened by wooden pins.

The most important type of early chair, however, was the joiner-made "close" or "sealed" chair of which many early examples were imported, probably from Flanders. This chair obviously evolved from the box or chest which served in many a home as seat, table, and bed. The back stiles of the panelled cupboard seat were elongated to support the solid panelling which, until about 1620, invariably formed the chair back (Page 54, Fig. 51). Arms were similarly added as a logical part of the construction. In many early sixteenth-century examples all the panels, like the backs of contemporary pew-like settles, were carved in Gothic linen-fold pattern, often combined with the Italianesque heads, figures, and scrolls of early Renaissance work; probably many were further enriched with paint.

Rarely, in Elizabethan days, the heavy box panels below the seat might be modified to show plainly rectangular legs linked by stretchers. But the panelled back was not so easily ousted. The top rail was usually tenoned into the side uprights: not until the early seventeenth century did it become customary for the rail to extend across and beyond the tops of the uprights as shaped cresting. The resultant wide "ear-piece" effect was then sometimes exaggerated and the scrolling bracket beneath it, attached to the outer side of each upright, became correspondingly important (Page 54, Fig. 52). But even then some chair-makers continued the earlier custom of fitting the cross-rail between the uprights, rejecting the ear-piece development.

The back uprights, moulded and somewhat raked, were still invariably continuations of the rear legs, which were flatly rectangular below the thin, flat seat. The front legs, however, by late in the sixteenth century, were being turned, often fluted (Page 56, Figs. 67, 68 and 69), in vase or baluster outline which escaped the exaggerated melon shapes seen on tables and early court cupboards.

Rather later came the various ball and reel forms of turning especially associated with the mid-seventeenth century (Page 56, Fig. 70). In both types the legs were left square—only their arrises rounded off—where construction necessitated mortise-and-tenon joints (Fig. 88). Early stretchers, broad and low set, were entirely rectangular, sometimes moulded. Above the seat, more turning decorated the continuations of the legs which supported the arms. These, although of rectangular section, were considerably shaped for comfort and finished with rounded ends. The

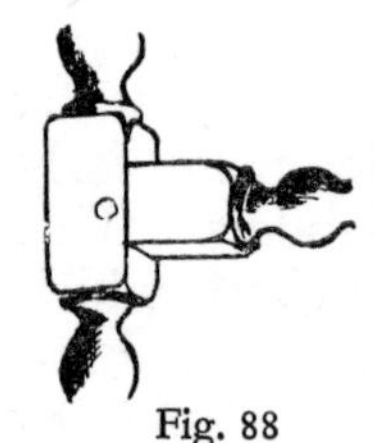

Fig. 88

This elm-wood chair dates to about 'oo and demonstrates the continuity ' the turner's construction methods om the earliest days of English chair-making.

b. An early Stuart oak chair, the cresting rail still framed-in between the back verticals. The solid panel back shows the arch motif and the stretchers are broad and low.

An Elizabethan stool for dining, solidly "joined" construction. ıe legs are splayed back and front for stability. About 1600.

d. The so-called "Yorkshire" chair dating from soon after the middle of seventeenth century, with horseshoe shaping to the carved rails. The heavy stretchers show typical reel turning.

a. A handsome late Charles II walnut chair, with amorini on the cresting and front stretcher. Details in the carving suggest that this may be Continental work.

b. In this walnut chair the caning h become less important, the design bei dominated by emphatic S-scrolls combin with the popular rose and crown motif.

c. An early example of the upholstered chair with wings and scrolling arms. Built for stability, the legs are left square for the mortise and tenon joints of the stretchers. William III.

d. This tall, raking back and the out-turn arms and front legs in the form of Flemi scrolls are typical of the James II peric

angle at which they were set into the back tended to become steeper as the period advanced.

These chairs were weighty, important pieces of furniture and their decoration was correspondingly handsome. Inlay was rare on chairs. More usual was the virile carving of the Elizabethan period which frequently included variants of the arcading particularly associated with Renaissance decoration. Heavy scroll designs formed an arched cresting to the top of the chair, balanced by smaller scrolling on the ear-pieces. By Stuart times, however, the carving was becoming stereotyped, elaborate instead of imaginative, and largely dependent on arched flutings, innumerable gouge cuts, the guilloche and similar conventional strapwork (Fig. 89).

Such solid panelled oak chair backs continued to appear in country work into the late seventeenth century, and it appears that the so-called monk's table on similar heavy lines was only developed during this century, although its form can be traced even to the early sixteenth century. One is mentioned in the 1624 inventory of Gilling Castle. In shape it was either a chair or settle with solid back and solid horizontal arms. The vertical back was tilted forward to rest upon these arms when a table was required. The name appears to have no significance: more explicit is the phrase in a mid-sixteenth century will quoted by E. W. Gregory, "a yoyned table, chayrewyse".

Fig. 89

The seventeenth century heralded a great impetus in chair production, chairs beginning to be made single as well as with arms. Admittedly even in noble houses of post-Restoration England stools were still much in evidence—many upholstered—and were the usual seat for meals; throughout most of the seventeenth century it was the fashion to make them *en suite* with the table. But Continental influences were becoming stronger, suggesting new methods and creating new demands. Among these figured the upholstered chair, not common until after 1660, in which over-stuffed seat and back were covered in fabric secured by brass-headed nails. Some were armchairs, some single, the latter including the so-called farthingale chair which dates from this century.

The effect of dress upon furniture is a fascinating study. Early chairs with their broad arms reflected the various fashions in heavy sleeves. The farthingale chair, with no arms, a wide and very high seat and strongly raked back, offered the most convenient support and finest display to that peculiar whalebone framing worn under the dress to achieve a hooped effect on the hips; this was the fashion as early as 1547 but became more exaggerated at the court of James I.

The upholstery itself on such a chair was obviously considered sufficient decoration at this period, plainly square back and seat being associated with turned legs and plain stretchers. Leather upholstery was particularly prominent during the Cromwellian period. It was originally a Spanish speciality, probably introduced from Africa by the Moors, but reached England by way of Holland which had long been at war with Spain.

The Cromwellian period is usually associated with plain furniture styles. It would probably be fairer to regard it as revealing, for lack of more extravagant foreign novelties among the leaders of fashion, the sturdy, homely work which was being produced throughout the century by the ordinary country makers.

One noticeable, if small, change at this period concerned the arrangement of chair stretchers. At each side there might now be two, while the front one, set much higher on the legs than in earlier work, was often turned. It was, in fact, no longer so essential as a footrest above the "marsh" of the floor, and its other purpose of strengthening the chair structure could be served equally well in a more decorative manner. Frequently on later Cromwellian work all stretchers were turned—most usually unimaginative ball turning—but were still left square for the mortise-and-tenon joints. The arms were generally straight and square, and, although the leather seat might be slung between the uprights, there was as yet no thought of shaping the framework to ease the sitter's back.

Another noteworthy development of the period was seen

on upholstered chairs. In many cases the padding extended little more than half way down the back uprights, leaving a space above the seat, sometimes edged with deep fringes to match the trimming around the seat itself. This tendency reflected the general trend of the times towards lighter chair styles. It was merely a transitional phase between solid panelling and open rails, but for some reason half-panelled, heavily carved backs happened to become firmly established in the north of England. After the mid-seventeenth century solid panelled backs were largely confined to traditional country work, but the low severely square back outlines usually dubbed "Cromwellian" were undoubtedly produced for many years after the Restoration.

One alternative to half-panelling on the backs of plain wooden chairs was to introduce several cross-rails. Most characterful examples of this period were the so-called Yorkshire and Derbyshire chairs (Page 54, Fig. 53). Many were made between 1640 and 1675 and are considered by some to show traces of Scandinavian influence. In these chairs the rails, usually two, showed many variations of rounded arches—some even the un-English horseshoe shape—often edged with smaller scalloping, and further ornamented with a number of upright and pendant acorns or knobs. In some the spaces between the rails contained vertical-turned spindles, occasionally also found linking seat rail and stretcher. More spindles were often split and glued to the faces of the chair uprights in the fashion of the day. In addition, carving in conventional scrolls, and sometimes even including a roughly executed human mask, completed the "foreign" and rather excessive ornamentation.

The uprights were topped with shaped or turned finials. Often these were inward curving volutes similar to those on the ear-pieces of panelled chairs. These chairs frequently followed the fashion of the mid-century of framing-in the seat boards instead of placing them on top of the rails: the result was a slightly sunken seat which would accommodate a flat cushion (Fig. 90).

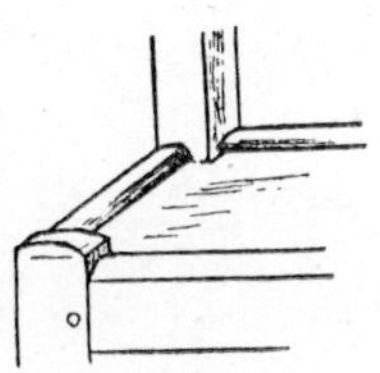

Fig. 90

The arm or single chair with turned rails,

back spindles, seat frame, and stretchers was still in vogue ten years after the Restoration. But a more conspicuous development was the first tentative effort to break away from the dull, heavy ball turning of the mid-century in favour of lighter spiral twists (Page 56, Fig. 71).

Turners had long found oak an intractable wood for their lathes and for spiral twists it proved particularly ill-suited, being brittle when cut across the grain. Early attempts were made to shape the spirals by hand, but it was the modification of the lathe to make oblique cuts—swash-turning—reaching this country from the Continent with the Restoration, that brought spiral twists into commercial use. And in any case in fashionable homes oak was beginning to give place, by then, to the more easily worked walnut. Indeed, post-Restoration oak chairs were soon but simple country cousins of prevailing walnut styles.

a. Interesting as a transitional form, this William III chair has a panel of carving, a cresting rail scrolling over the uprights, and front legs showing a tentative approach to the new form shown in (b) and (c). The front stretcher suggests strong Continental influence.

.n upholstered stool in walnut. :gs, with mushroom swelling at and ankle height, and its well-ded "tied" diagonal stretchers date from the 1690's.

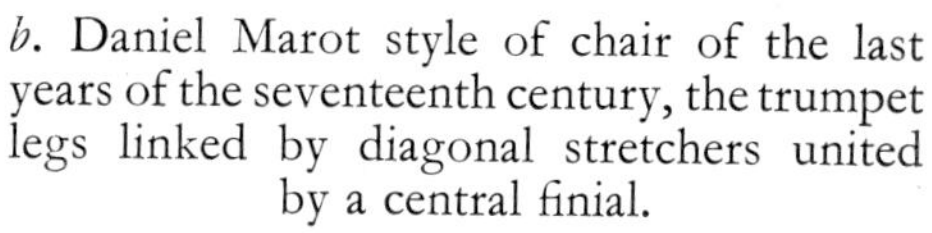

b. Daniel Marot style of chair of the last years of the seventeenth century, the trumpet legs linked by diagonal stretchers united by a central finial.

PLATE 11

a. New features introduced from abroad around the close of the seventeenth century included a central splat shaped to fit the sitter's back. These early cabriole legs retain their stretchers and have hoof feet.

b. These plainly rounded outlines are typi of innumerable early-eighteenth-centu upholstered walnut chairs. Back as well front legs are in cabriole outline. Queen An

c. Here the legs have become slightly squat, carved on the knees and mounted on ball-and-claw feet, while the back splat has lost all carving and piercing. Early Georgian.

5

CHAIRS OF THE WALNUT PERIOD

WALNUT chairs, and the stools that underwent very similar development, are associated especially with the years 1660-1730. As early as 1558, however, an inventory recorded a chair of walnut "sett with boneworke", and during Cromwellian days that lovely wood, so long appreciated for superfine furniture, was being called unostentatiously into the chair-maker's service.

This comparatively austere period, when the country chair-maker was undisturbed by demands for new-fangled Continental notions, was dominated by variants of repetitive knob, ball, and bobbin turnery on all the rails, uprights, and stretchers of chairs. Inevitably their monotony prompted attempts at the more ambitious twist turning (Page 56, Fig. 71), known in Holland and Portugal since 1600 and in Italy still earlier. But oak, it was found, was too brittle for such antics, while solid walnut, and to some extent the cheaper beech wood, proved considerably more amenable.

At first these spirals were laboriously cut by hand, but soon after 1660 the so-called swash-turning came into use, in which oblique curves could be achieved with the aid of a slide rest on the lathe. Between 1660 and 1665 the twist turn was introduced as freely and enthusiastically as the earlier knob turning. Twist-turned back uprights ended in turned knob finials, and legs and rails were only left in square section, with rounded arrises, where security demanded mortise-and-tenon joints.

Twist-turned chairs in the fulness of their development were typical of the vast change from Cromwellian to

Restoration England: the contrast between solid country work on more or less traditional lines and a gradual absorption of Continental ideas, at first often little more than superficially understood. Italy, Spain, France, Flanders, and Holland contributed to the chaotic exuberance that characterized the later years of the seventeenth century, and there can be no single definition of the Restoration chair. But, typically, the twist-turned back uprights were still unbroken continuations of the back legs, now set at a considerable rake which by 1680-90 was a definite constructional weakness in single chairs. The top rail, set between the uprights, was plainly rectangular, or at most showed light moulding on the edges. The arms, flat and tenoned into the back uprights and into extensions of the front legs, were shaped in outward bows.

The seat rails were of rectangular section, occasionally showing incised geometrical decoration. The front stretcher was placed half-way up the twist-turned front legs which were based on ball or vase-turned feet. It would appear that for some years the low, square back of the previous period continued in favour, whether composed of turned spindles or a panel of upholstery. Not for some time came that most conspicuous development, the caning of back and seat, in fulfilment of another tentative Cromwellian experiment. But within a century, in 1761, Joseph Collyer could refer to "cane being now entirely out of use".

At first, this weight-saving material was coarse, in an open mesh. On the caned seat, the walnut framing was sometimes strengthened with an inner lining of oak; on the back the caning was confined to a panel—elliptical in some of the finest examples—framed by the top and base cross-rails and by inner side verticals which were unconnected with the main side uprights of the chair (Page 54, Fig. 54). Alternatively a chair might show a back composed of a row of flat vertical wooden splats, sometimes, at just this period, shaped to suggest the silhouette of twist turning, and a seat of rush work. But caning was so popular in William's reign that woollen manufacturers petitioned the king to place a ban on the material which was ousting their upholstery fabrics.

Before the end of Charles' reign, French-Italian influence was becoming expressed more strongly on the backs of chairs. On the rails and the inner side-pieces that held the caning, crude, flattish carving made its appearance, at first little more than a crown, rose, or acanthus leaf motif. This was repeated on the broad front face of the front stretcher which now resembled the top rail—a rectangular board, four or five inches deep (Fig. 91).

Fig. 91

Soon, however, the carving was immeasurably improved, the background pierced, and the motifs presented in high relief with particular delight in *amorini* supporting crowns, flowers, or family crests. As treatment became more confident and fluent, outlines became freer. The top rail at the back was still held between restrictive side uprights, but both this and the front stretcher (Fig. 92) curved upwards in a central arch, often formed of opposing S-scrolls.

This was the great period for S-scroll design in England. But, far from being peculiar to the Stuart régime, this satisfying and well-balanced if rather flamboyant line was to be found also in Flanders, Holland, France, and Spain. Richly and sharply curved, it constituted the front leg design of many chairs, especially between 1675 and 1690 (Page 56, Fig. 72). Usually it paralleled the side of the chair but sometimes flared outwards at an over-emphatic angle. It was often to be found also in the supports to the chair arms.

Fig. 92

The arm horizontals, now in rounded section, paralleled the straight sides of the chair but dipped slightly in the centre for greater comfort, and often scrolled over their supports in extravagant outward curves. The arms were sometimes lightly carved: on rich examples the seat rail and even the solid rectangular blocks on the various rails that held the mortise-and-tenon joints were incised with simple patterns such as flowers and foliage. With these S-scrolls to the front of the chair was often combined a wealth of twist turning on back uprights and stretchers, but an alternative now was the less exuberant baluster turning. In any case twist turning had almost disappeared from fashionable chairs in favour of baluster turning by James II's reign, long before it was abandoned on table legs.

It was at this period that the couch or day-bed began to become important. It was known earlier: in the early seventeenth century it might be an elaborate canopied, curtained affair "with a bayes cover to the seate", or an upholstered settle design with adjustable ends. Indeed a simple settee is featured in the fourteenth-century Longthorpe Tower wall paintings referred to in more detail in Chapter 9. But it was the increased differentiation between living and sleeping apartments that prompted its development, and the advent of caning that resulted in a really light, convenient article. One end resembled a contemporary chair-back and the seat extended on six or more legs linked by the typical wide "front" stretcher all along the side. Shaping of the back for greater comfort seems to have appeared notably earlier on day-beds than on chairs. This style of day-bed was the forerunner of the chaise-longue which, when given a second "back" at the other end, became the "duchesse" of the later eighteenth century.

By the end of Charles II's reign caning was of finer mesh, but many chairs were then being made with padded backs, very many more with padded seats. In wholly upholstered chairs the back and seat framing were entirely hidden in over-stuffing covered with velvet, richly fringed, with damasks or other silken beauty. Less expensive chairs were given charming individuality with hand embroidery or with tapestries from the Mortlake establishment. Fringed, upholstered stools were known as tabourets.

Typical of the newest fashion in James II's reign were exuberantly carved chairs, with backs ornately crested between the turned uprights. These expressed a French mode which became more marked in the last decade of the century, during the general transition from Spanish and

Flemish styles to the Dutch adaptations of the French Louis XIV fashions, basically derived from the Italians. In some notably French examples the whole central panel of the back consisted of rich pierced carving.

Until this period the seats on English chairs had followed the well-proved construction method in which the four side rails were mortised into the sides of the back and front legs (Fig. 93A). Now, as a less substantial alternative, some chairs were made with the front legs let into holes bored in the seat corners (Fig. 93B); the seat, broad, thinner than on Continental work and often showing a round-moulded edge, was built up into a complete unit before being let into the sides of the back uprights. At this time, too, the cresting rail went through a similar constructional change. This development, however, was far from new, being but a repetition of a change witnessed in oak chairs early the same century: the back cresting was made to ride upon the tops of the uprights instead of being held by horizontal mortise-and-tenon joints between them (Page 54, Fig. 55).

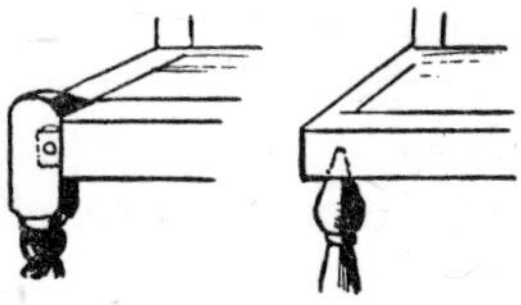

A Fig. 93 B

In William's reign it was obviously from Holland that innovation was to be expected, but Huguenot and French influence also contributed to the chair fashions of the 1690's. Carving on the cresting tended to become simpler and that on the front stretcher, now some version of a moulded arch, similarly reduced, although often executed in full relief, in conventional scrolls or a leaf pattern.

The greater rake to the back necessitated a corresponding slant to the back legs. The panels of superfine caning took many ornamental shapes with arched or ogee-moulded top and base, but all emphasized the tall and narrow lines responsible for the name periwig chairs. In some cases the caning, when not ousted by upholstered padding, was no more than a narrow strip between wide panels of full-relief carving.

Legs and feet also expressed the general tendency to confusion in furniture of the period. Most conspicuous among leg forms was decorative baluster turning with a swelling "Portuguese" bulb (Page 56, Fig. 73) or slightly later mushroom shape near the top, tapering to a rounded or cup-shaped foot. But scroll shapes had not yet disappeared, and the fluted projecting club or "Spanish" foot (Fig. 94) continued prominent.

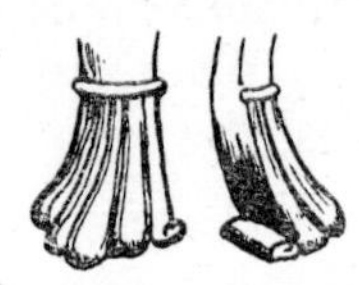

Fig. 94

In the underframing, an innovation of the period was the use of diagonally placed stays instead of the well-proved arrangement of stretchers paralleling the edges of the chair. These stays were framed into blocks on the legs immediately above the feet and met under the centre of the chair, where they were most usually tenoned into a central block or were lap-halved where they crossed and "tied" by a peg with a neatly-turned finial (Fig. 95). Indeed, the whole method was confined to high-quality work. A carved apron was occasionally introduced under the seat rail, and the stays themselves, shaped in scrolling designs, were moulded and often elaborately carved—but were graceful rather than efficient.

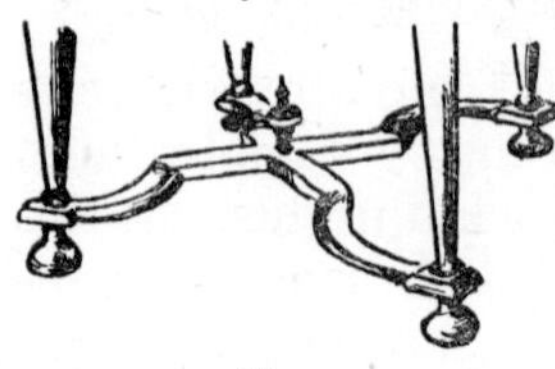

Fig. 95

Although walnut was the accepted wood for quality work, before the end of the century there was much imitation of Oriental lacquer. This gradually deteriorated: by 1800 there were many unpretentious little black painted chairs in beechwood which, like elm, maple, or a mixture of woods, was chosen where it was easily obtained. On upholstered chairs such wood as was left uncovered was often gilded over heavy carving.

Upholstery was by now a normal part of the chair-maker's business and the "upholder's" products included the "sleeping chair", rare until the eighteenth century, with forward-jutting wings at the top of the back curving down to the outward-scrolling arms. Some of these chairs had adjustable backs worked by iron ratchets.

The last years of the seventeenth century were strongly influenced by the house and furniture designer Daniel Marot, whose Huguenot family had fled to Holland and who worked for William III. Couches, and chairs with tall upholstered backs, are most associated with his masterly, if somewhat florid, blending of French and Dutch styles, but some chairs showed backs composed entirely of lavish pierced carving between the uprights. Caning also continued on chair backs but, like upholstery, covered the whole back instead of being confined to a narrow central panel.

Carving on the handsome upsweeping cresting was repeated on the front stretcher, often set back from the front legs and tenoned instead into the side stretchers, which might themselves follow a waved outline (Fig. 96). Front legs often showed square moulding and such geometrical forms as octagonal or rounded "mushrooms" (Page 56, Figs. 74 and 75) tapering to less swelling octagonal feet, an outline much associated with this period and found, for example, in such details as the shouldered stems of contemporary wine glasses.

Fig. 96

Such enrichment, however, was as nothing in the evolution of chair design when compared with the basic change that took place at the close of the seventeenth century—the change from predominantly straight lines to a wholly new insistence upon curves. This found expression in the hooped back, in curving silhouette (Page 54, Fig. 56); in the frequent serpentine seat framing; even in a shaped apron to the seat rail; and most conspicuously of all in the cabriole leg (Page 56, Fig. 76), a form which so manifestly demanded the abandonment of all forms of stretcher that for nearly fifty years their use was restricted to work intended for farmhouse and cottage.

These changes were gradual, but their evolution entirely dominated chair construction throughout the rest of the walnut period.

At first on the un-upholstered chair, the back tended to retain the parallel side uprights, now flat instead of turned and overtopped by arched cresting carved on more formal lines. Between them, instead of a panel of caning or upholstery, rose a wide central wooden splat, framed by cresting and bottom rail. Often at this time this was carved and pierced, although the essentially Dutch fashion for smooth-surfaced marquetry was reducing the demand for carved furniture.

The principal change in construction, however, was the consideration for comfort shown in the curve that rippled down the whole chair back: convex at the nape of the sitter's neck, concave to rest his shoulders, convex again to fit the small of his back. This shaping, revealing the end-grain in the wood, required a covering of veneer. At the same time, the square lines of the seat, frequently over-stuffed, might be softened with a curving-front apron. And the legs, while still introducing ornate stretchers—waved at the sides and crested at the front, in the Marot style—might adopt the curve of the cabriole leg.

Around 1700, this ancient design, that expressed to perfection in its assured curves the poise and "spring" of an animal's hind leg, was frequently given the hoof foot (Fig. 97) and a definite suggestion of a hock. Its development could not be considered complete, however, until it was rid of the distracting cross lines of stretchers, early in the eighteenth century. And by then the hoof foot was being modified to the most usual pad or club foot (Page 57, Fig. 77). The more decorative ball-and-claw foot (Page 57, Fig. 78) dates more especially from 1710 onwards, when either eagle's claw or lion's paw might be represented, its "grip" upon the ball the mark of a skilled craftsman. Like the contemporary fashion for escallop shell carving on the knee of the leg, it had long been in use on the Continent.

Fig. 97

English made cabriole legs were noted for their particularly fine proportions. They were by no means simple to make: indeed, they must still be shaped largely by hand. J. C. Rogers has described the method in detail. First, the general outline had to be cut with a bow saw from a length of close-grained wood. This included a block above the knee into which the seat rails could be tenoned. Occasionally a chair leg was left in square section, but far more usually the next operation consisted in lathe-turning the pad foot (if used) and then applying spokeshave and rasp to reduce

A typical late Charles II
-bed in walnut and cane,
cresting and four broad
etchers showing the
ɔrini-and-crown decora-
ı which dominated this
period.

b. A William and Mary upholstered example of the love-seat, with tall back, trumpet-shaped legs, Spanish feet and diagonal stretchers.

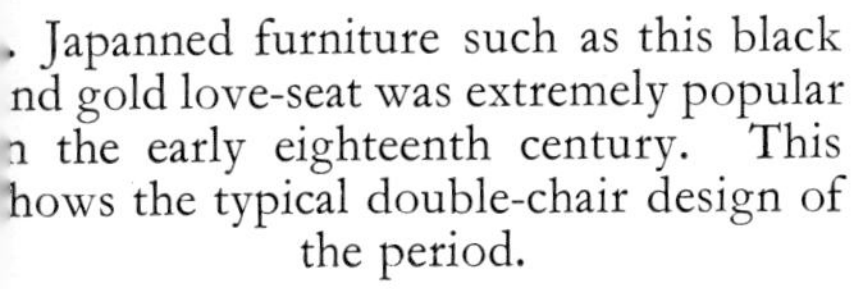

. Japanned furniture such as this black
nd gold love-seat was extremely popular
ı the early eighteenth century. This
hows the typical double-chair design of
the period.

a. A mahogany chair typical of the rich carving of the George I period. The splat is carved but not pierced. The back legs are in cabriole profile.

b. A mahogany roundabout particularly well-shaped seat, cabriole legs on ball-and-claw About 1740.

c. This mahogany chair of about 1750 has the cupid's bow cresting, a splat still noticeably flat, and arms carved with eagles' heads.

d. The mid-eighteenth-century maho chair at its best, with carved and pie splat, resembling designs publishec Chippendale, Ince and Mayhew, others.

Mahogany chair in the "Gothic" anner of around 1760, with "Gothic indow" shaping instead of the central splat.

b. This mahogany "Chinese" chair has square-cut trellis back and arms. The wave-moulded legs have plain stretchers. About 1760.

A finely carved example of the ahogany ladder-back. Egg-and-dart oulding edges the square straight legs.

d. A ribband-backed chair showing the perfection of the carver's skill with mahogany, around 1755-60. The front legs are on scroll feet.

a. An upholstered chair in the Louis XVI style favoured by Adam, with upholstery on the arm horizontals. The fluted legs are tapered and all exposed wood is gilded.

b. This gilded chair dates to the last ye of the eighteenth century. The back suggestive of contemporary mirror fram surrounding a typical painted nosegay.

c. This chair in the Adam style expresses another French fashion—the splat carved to resemble a lyre, with metal strings. About 1775.

d. Dating to the Hepplewhite period, this chair has legs in the "French cabriole" style with contempo castors on barrel-like "rollers".

the arrises to rounded section. The knee was frequently left rough for carving.

At each side above the knee and immediately below the seat framing, the leg still ended abruptly in a vertical face. This might be left untouched or finished with an applied motif. In later work it was more usually given a small shoulder at each side, continuing the curve of the leg. This might be dowelled or glued into position, but in either case did not contribute much to the strength of the construction. Any carving, such as foliage, on the knee was extended on the shoulders with unifying effect.

As stretchers became discarded from the cabriole leg design, the strain-resistance of the seat framing became a matter of greater importance. Indeed, heavy upholstered armchairs with cabriole legs long retained their stretchers. Seat rails, usually moulded on their top edges, had to be made deep enough to be tenoned into the blocks left at the tops of the legs. Sometimes, however, a thin, upholstered drop-in seat was introduced; and the upper half of each seat rail had then to be reduced in thickness to receive it. Additional strengthening of the joints between seat rail and legs was achieved by screwing in triangular blocks which also often helped to support the loose seat (Fig. 98). Under over-stuffed upholstery the seat rails might be of oak or beech instead of walnut and some were reinforced with open braces.

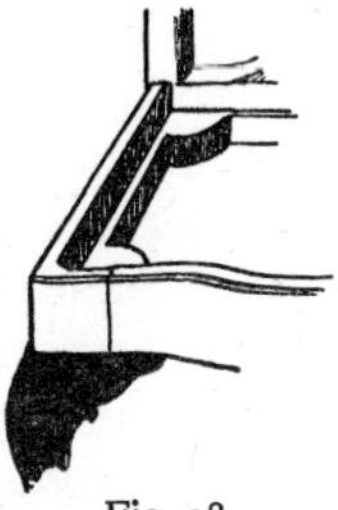

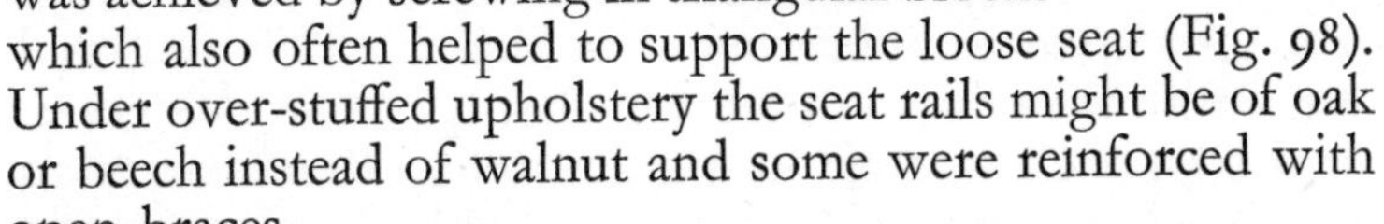

Fig. 98

At first only the front legs followed the cabriole line and often joined the seat frame without the flared shaping of shoulder pieces. The rear legs were square at first and later more often turned in plain round section. The finest followed the cabriole line. Club feet (Fig. 99) on these legs and the absence of stretchers date a chair to late in Queen Anne's reign or later.

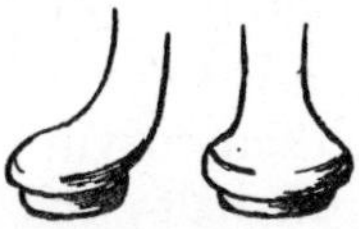

Fig. 99

While legs were losing their stretchers, backs were losing their parallel uprights in favour of hooped shapes. The cresting rail, arched and sometimes carved, was but an uninterrupted continuation of the sides. By

Queen Anne's reign these side uprights had developed into long S-curves under somewhat dished cresting (Page 54, Fig. 57); they broke away from the vertical a few inches above the seat in a shoulder effect, still traceable in some of Chippendale's early work near the middle of the eighteenth century. Framed into the cresting and either the bottom rail or more usually the back of the seat, the splat now also showed edges shaped in curving outlines. Narrower, with perhaps no more than its edges delicately carved, and seldom pierced, it was given something of the outline of a violin. The danger of meaningless in-and-out shaping was not always avoided, however, in either fiddle or somewhat later baluster and vase designs.

During the Queen Anne period the straight upright was not entirely lost, but was restricted to austerely simple chairs. The slender uprights of the tall back were in rounded section, joined squarely to the top rail with no more than the corners rounded off. The pleasing effect was increased by the splat, plain in outline, and sometimes given individuality with a panel of marquetry.

Contemporary, too, was the development of the curving seat frame which was not, however, invariably used. By 1700 the two front corners were being rounded; then the front rail was shaped in a simple inward or outward curve or a serpentine combination; then the side rails followed suit. With the change in the seat framing came changes in the design of chair arms. Displaying yet another break from traditional practice, they were no longer supported on continuations of the front legs but were set back several inches from the broad front of the chair, allowing more space for the panniered dresses of the day. Typical Queen Anne work was the arm shaped in one continuous curve, flat and slightly dished and outward curving on the horizontal, then curving sharply downwards in a full half-circle to a serpentine vertical (Fig. 100). This arm was often in square section where it was framed into the back upright, the rest in round section until it broadened

Fig. 100

out to be attached to the outside of the side seat-rail. An alternative was the arm form in which the horizontal bar ended in a carved scroll or volute projecting beyond the vertical support. This was a Restoration mode never entirely lost which lent itself to elaborate carving, but lions' heads and the like were more particularly a fashion of subsequent Georgian mahogany furniture.

Similar arm forms were introduced on the love seats that came into fashion late in Queen Anne's reign (early upholtered examples may date from the end of the seventeenth century). The design suggested a fusion of two armchairs, retaining the outer arms, the double arching back with two splats, the outer legs and, in the centre, only one pair of legs. The central cabriole knee was thus particularly prominent; it was often finely carved and set between waved and occasionally carved front aprons.

It must be remembered that the popular upholstery was now by no means restricted to armchairs. While winged grandfather chairs with scroll-over arms were becoming more numerous, many single chairs were being made with back and seat entirely upholstered. For these, velvet or colourful needlework provided ample decoration; on exposed wood of other chairs various new decorative media were employed with handsome effect. For many, cross-grain walnut veneer on back and seat rails, with particularly fine veneer on the central splat, offered opportunities for displaying the lovely wood in a way impossible on the solid of the legs. More ornate were splats decorated with marquetry. Japanning has already been mentioned; still more lavish was gilded gesso, dating principally between 1700 and 1735 and producing finely moulded motifs on cresting, splat, seat-rail, and knees.

Simple but effective was the carved decoration. On Queen Anne chairs this was light and more restricted than in early Georgian work. Gone were the crowns and cupids of Restoration days. Instead, the dominant motif was the very Dutch escallop shell, often with a husk at its base. When carving was applied to a veneered surface great skill was needed to ensure concealment of the join where the wood to be carved was glued over the veneer.

Such then was the evolution in chair design that dominated the walnut period, so complete that the Charles II chair seems to belong to another world, so lasting that the gradual adoption of the new wood, mahogany, only brought it greater enrichment. Indeed, when that eminent portrayer of life *à la mode*, William Hogarth, executed a self-portrait in 1764, the chair on which he was seated was of a type which might have been made forty or fifty years before.

6

CHAIRS OF THE MAHOGANY PERIOD

ENGLISH walnut furniture received a check in 1720 when the French put an embargo upon the export of the wood. But articles of Virginian walnut (*juglans nigra*) were specifically advertised in the 1730's, and walnut chairs in particular continued to be made for boudoir and bedroom in the middle years of the century when mahogany was attaining its greatest popularity. The early eighteenth century was marked by greatly increased comfort in ordinary homes where chairs of walnut, oak, and japanned or stained indigenous soft woods proved wholly satisfactory. Only a rich minority followed such fashion leaders as William Kent who devised heavily architectural furniture for their Palladian mansions.

Until 1733 high duties on imported timber severely limited the use of the weighty new mahogany. As far as possible it was applied as a thin veneer over such native woods as oak and beech; many a mahogany chair is found with even the back seat-rail of veneered beechwood. Early mahogany veneers, however, lacked the rich grain patterns of walnut. The early Santo Domingo wood showed a glowing tone, but figured Cuban mahogany veneers came into full use only in the second half of the century.

One important result was a change of emphasis from surface decorations to proportions and outlines. Built-up gesso work, of necessity gilded or silvered, was already established as an ultra-lavish fashion, but the dense growth of the early mahogany prompted the development of more satisfying carving. In form, as was shown in the previous chapter, chairs had undergone a revolutionary change at the beginning of the century. Until the 1740's the majority of early Georgian chairs followed established lines, merely becoming weightier and more extensively carved with shells, scrolls, and the like on cresting, splat, seat-rail, and cabriole knee; even the foot was often enriched with strongly-carved ball-and-claw or lion's paw (Page 57, Fig. 78).

By the 1720s the claw talons might be of brass or the whole leg naturalistically carved to resemble a lion's—and then perhaps made almost ludicrous by the introduction of shell and husk carved on the knee and perhaps a satyr's mask upon the seat-rail. The heavy, fiercely realistic carving of this period has been attributed to late Renaissance feeling in Germany, brought to England by the Hanoverians. It took hold during the period of experiment and extensive Continental borrowing that marked the transition from Queen Anne walnut to Chippendale mahogany.

In general outline the early Georgian chair-back tended to show less rounded cresting rail, squarer corners. The uprights followed a gradual inward curve down to the seat in place of the earlier shoulder effect a little above it. The back legs curved inwards a little and backwards considerably, ending in club feet.

On armchairs the projecting horizontals offered further opportunities for lions' heads, Cerberus heads and similar carving, facing straight ahead or curving outwards. Even on many upholstered chairs the arms were wholly exposed or padded only on the horizontals: in either case the carved vertical supports swept up and back in steep curves leaving ample space for the vast dresses of the period. Needlework and damask upholsteries were plentiful and some mohair was used.

At this period many upholstered grandfather chairs were made, but it is rare to find grandfather and grandmother chairs forming a pair, the latter being the wider and somewhat lower. After 1730 the backs of all upholstered chairs tended to become lower, the cabriole legs decidedly squat. Lions' masks frequently ornamented the low knees, the "lion period" dating particularly, but by no means rigidly, to the years 1720-35, and satyr masks to 1730-40. By 1740 both were giving way to a greater use of acanthus leaf carving—acknowledgment of the classic trend in the architects' furniture of the wealthy.

The latter was designed for such a limited clientele that it never became a commercial vogue, but passing reference may be made to lavish carving on chairs of mahogany and walnut picked out with gilt and of soft woods wholly gilded. William Kent gave his early chairs heavy S-scroll legs; his cabrioles were finished with French scroll feet—caricatured in Laroon's conversation pieces of the 1730's. Some of the most elaborate legs in Kent's style showed eagles' heads supporting swags of flowers and fruit. Below the rich damask or velvet seat the rail might be carved with such classic motifs as the key pattern (Fig. 101) and Vitruvian scroll (Fig. 102) favoured by Robert Adam much later in the century when the real classic revival came to be expressed in furniture. Some very ornate japanned chairs of this period must also be remembered. These are especially associated with the Clerkenwell district where Giles Grendey (1693-1780)—one of the few who labelled his furniture—is known to have worked for a considerable home and export market.

Fig. 101

Fig. 102

It was in the less architectural, "French" period of the 1740's, however, that the English chair began to express the individuality of mahogany in a distinctive manner. By then even the classic acanthus leaf was lighter and less formal and was introduced, for example, to edge the scrolling outline of the chair splat, carved out of wood glued to the splat edges. The wealth of French rococo decoration introduced at this period may seem almost excessive by English standards, but it suited both the chair form and the prevailing medium far better than the painted ornament that predominated at the close of the century. The inevitable rub of use only enhanced the carving, cut with a metallic brilliance from the hard Spanish mahogany.

In many chairs of the period the splat still held to the Queen Anne fiddle outline but now consisted of a flat pierced design, finely interlaced strapwork, scrolls and the like, adapted from the French *rocaille* work of Meissonier and others, and even touched with gilt on specifically "French" examples. Thomas Chippendale was but one enthusiast among many with a keen eye for business among the rich men of fashion.

For the period 1745-60, then, the typical chair was in mahogany, the richer examples crisply carved on back-rails and splat, on arms, seat-rails and legs; the less elaborate showing no more than a little rococo work on the crest-rail and C-scroll or strapwork on the splat above plain cabriole legs. The typical crest-rail showed the cupid's bow outline ascribed to Chippendale but perhaps evolved a little earlier, the sides of the bow most usually meeting the verticals in small upward curves (Page 55, Fig. 58).

On the splat the early flat strapwork gave place to more deeply carved ribband treatment embodying elaborate scrolls and leaf carving and chisel-trimmed on the back for greater lightness (Page 55, Fig. 59). The daring pierced curves swept up into the lines of the crest-rail to resemble a single piece of wood. Occasionally and not too successfully the ribband motifs linked the splat to the side uprights; usually the air of solidity was emphasised by a splat firmly based on the back seat-rail.

On the centre of the crest-rail Chippendale might introduce the French *cabochon* motif used more generally on the cabriole knee. Other cabriole knees showed leaf carving which scrolled across the wavy outline of the serpentine frame. But many seat-rails of chairs and settees—which were often of the two- or three-chair variety—were square, perhaps edged with gadrooning (Fig. 103). The seat itself, tapering from front to back, might be stuffed-over or of the drop-in type: Chippendale himself suggested red morocco leather for some ribband-back chairs.

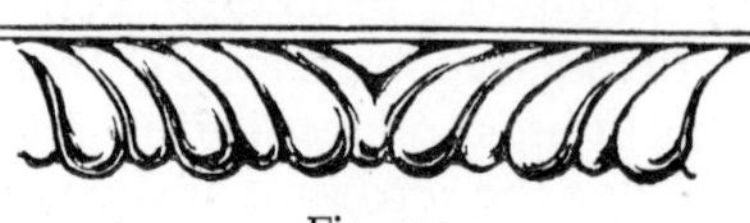

Fig. 103

Cabriole legs were now becoming lighter, less pronounced

a. With flower painting on its shield back, sloping arms and tapering legs, this style of chair was immensely popular in the last decades of the eighteenth century.

b. A late Sheraton period chair with broad cresting rail riding over the side uprights, S-shaped arms, and splayed legs.

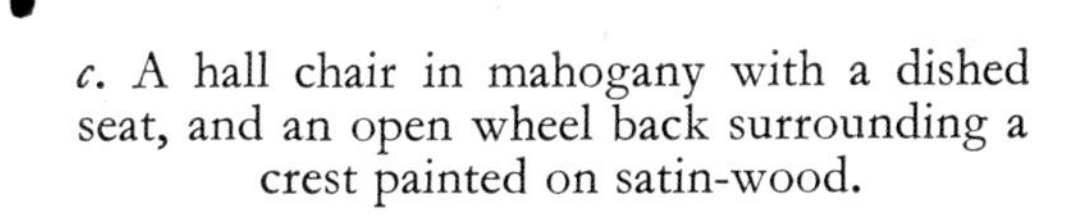

c. A hall chair in mahogany with a dished seat, and an open wheel back surrounding a crest painted on satin-wood.

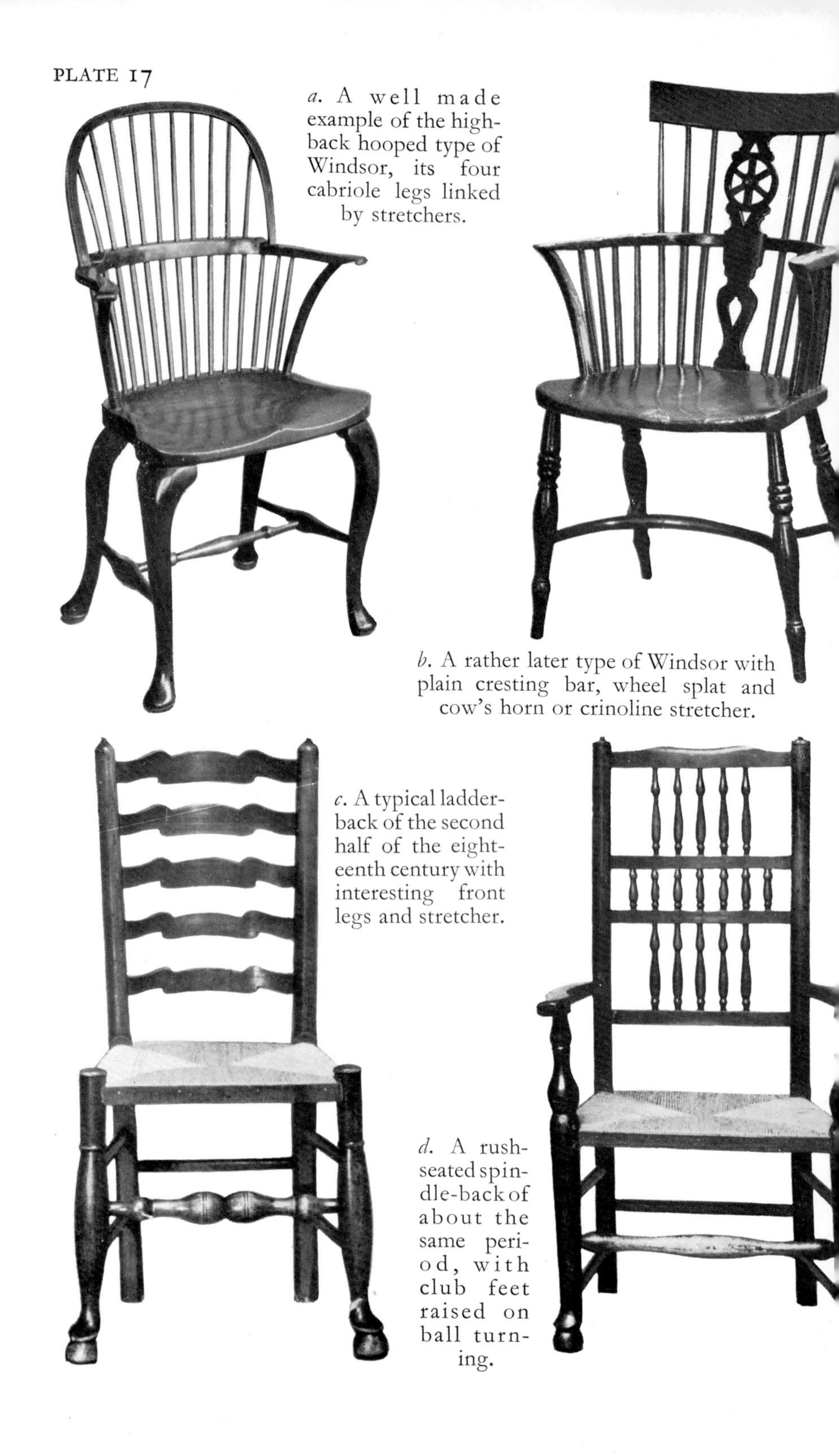

a. A well made example of the high-back hooped type of Windsor, its four cabriole legs linked by stretchers.

b. A rather later type of Windsor with plain cresting bar, wheel splat and cow's horn or crinoline stretcher.

c. A typical ladder-back of the second half of the eighteenth century with interesting front legs and stretcher.

d. A rush-seated spindle-back of about the same period, with club feet raised on ball turning.

than earlier work. Indeed, the whole outline to seat and legs was markedly lively (Page 57, Fig. 80), with dainty scroll or knurl toes. Chippendale's book of furniture designs published in 1754 suggested alternative cabriole or square legs for some chairs, but the date marks the decline of the cabriole leg which, by the last quarter of the century, was only to be found in a slender version on a few "French" Adam chairs. The return of the less expensive square lines, often with accompanying stretchers, was associated especially with the Chinese and Gothic moods that all too soon absorbed Chippendale and his contemporaries during the middle years of the century.

These craftsmen naturally caught hold of any passing fashion that might create new furniture demands. In chairs they introduced lattice backs and square legs, even pagoda-shaped cresting-rails. The lattice back abandoned all suggestion of a central splat, its vertical, horizontal, and diagonal trellis (Page 55, Fig. 61) entirely filling the space between uprights and cresting-rail, and between splayed arm horizontals and seat when arms were introduced. This trellis might be built up piece by piece or fret-cut from a single board as only mahogany could be. A strip of mahogany with low-relief fret-carving, called card-cut work—cut out of the solid wood in the best quality examples—might front the seat frame, or the frame might be pierced with the fret-cut design. It was usual to introduce fret-cut brackets at the angles between the seat frame and the square front legs (Page 57, Fig. 81). The legs themselves were either solid, with card-cut ornament, or L-shaped in section with fret-cut piercing, and sometimes reinforced with plainly turned verticals inside the L angles. Small plinth blocks might serve as feet and further fret-work ornamented the rectangular stretchers.

The "Gothic revival" prompted the production of chair backs with ogee arches and window tracery (Page 55, Fig. 62), often in incongruous association with cabriole legs and ball-and-claw feet. Even when square straight legs became established the French decorative touches of the '40s were still used with the Gothic work. Perhaps the most fitting legs were the cluster-column type, without stretchers, ending in small plinths. Other legs were five-sided.

Chinese fret styles were sometimes applied to settees and even occasionally to high-backed, winged chairs that would need many cushions to make them at all "easy". Gothic designs of similar severity lent themselves to the austere dignity of the dining room. For reading and writing, by Georgian days, a more homely little chair had been evolved, often found in walnut. This was the corner chair or roundabout, reminiscent of the old Dutch burgomaster chair of which specimens, often made in the Orient, are sometimes found in this country. The distinctive feature of the English chair was the placing of one corner to the front, often with a particularly well-shaped cabriole leg. The other three legs continued perhaps twelve inches above the seat and were linked by a horizontal rail, broader towards the centre, to form a comfortably supporting back, more or less semi-circular, the spaces between the uprights filled with two splats. The seat was most usually upholstered and of the drop-in variety. The legs might all be in cabriole shape or all but the front one square.

Such chairs are to be found with bookrest and candlestick attachments. Others, with similar low, rounded backs, were often called barbers' or shaving chairs, names that figured frequently in furniture sales of the early eighteenth century. But the terms were apparently loosely applied and the design modified to suit individual requirements. Some even showed the Windsor chair construction of the legs independent of the back uprights, taper-tenoned into a solid wooden saddle seat.

Yet another eighteenth century fashion of limited range was the ugly straddling chair designed with narrow back and strongly raking back legs for the richly-coated beau who sat astride it "back to front". Sometimes the back was padded at the top and extended for elbow rests. The poet John Gay is reputed to have possessed an example equipped with bookrest, candlestand, and, in the seat, a drawer for manuscripts. Sheraton illustrated a couple of very French examples, their cresting rails broadened to serve as elbow rests (Page 55, Fig. 65). A form with higher back was used by the judges of cocking mains.

A chair design of the period credited to Chippendale, although developed rather than originated by his firm, was the ladder-back, long favoured by country chairmakers. This was more elaborate than the rush-seated Dutch ladder-back, which will be considered separately among country chairs. The finest version, dating from about 1760, had a series of cross-rails running between the back uprights, following the slightly undulating line of the cresting rail (Page 55, Fig. 60). Often the cross-rails were pierced, in good examples the piercings being bordered with carving. Uprights and arm supports were often wave-moulded, the seat, over-stuffed or drop-in, often shaped to a rounded dip in the centre. As on other simple mahogany chairs, the legs were plainly square, or at most the front pair modified by simple wave-moulding on the outer sides, or showed such decoration on the outer arrises as narrow convex moulding or rope or bead carving.

Not until the late 1760's did chairs begin to shake free of the various trends expressed by many of Chippendale's contemporaries such as Manwaring and the firm of Ince and Mayhew. Incidentally, the latter called chairs with pierced backs "parlour chairs" and for chairs with upholstered backs clung to the old term "back stools".

The principal exponent of a new style of chair was the architect Robert Adam, who was not above designing chairs to suit the great houses he planned. Adam was deeply influenced by his travels in Italy and Dalmatia and by discoveries at Pompeii and Herculaneum. But it must be remembered, too, that France as well as England experienced a classic revival: much that was introduced here by Adam and his followers was doubtless suggested by England's obvious eighteenth century fashion leader across the Channel.

Adam chairs were usually small and fine, with low, narrow backs. Early examples were little more than modifications of the mid-century style. The crest-rail, for example, followed the typical bow line, but was delicately moulded; the splat was lightened, most conspicuously in the French-inspired lyre shape with its metal "strings" (Page 55,

Fig. 63); the leg, whether square or rounded in section, became tapering.

The previous decades' superabundance of carving would but detract from the studied grace in Adam outlines, which were soon modified to more curving profiles, the back in particular taking various oval, looping lines. In some cases the splat still rose from the back seat-rail but this, too, was a legacy of the previous fashion, and by the time Hepplewhite was producing his oval and shield-back chairs the splat was almost invariably contained entirely within the curved shape, and unconnected with the seat-rail. Often the oval back was upholstered within a moulded wooden frame. The rails of the oval or circular seat might be entirely covered with upholstery, but when uncovered were often carved with the Vitruvian scroll which, like seat caning, was a fashion reintroduced by Adam. Even the tapestry coverings showed classical detail, and the exposed wood, whether carved in low relief, inlaid or painted, offered endless opportunities for Adam's favourite classical motifs. The seat rails below the upholstery were linked by square blocks at the tops of the front legs and often showed sunken panels on which typical ornament included carved pateræ (Page 57, Figs. 82, 83). The square front legs on Adam mahogany chairs usually tapered without interruption from seat-rail to small moulded plinths, plain flutings emphasizing their slenderness.

Taper-turned legs were associated with upholstered chairs. Those at the back rose above the seat a few inches to support the oval upholstered back; those at the front rose above the seat as in an earlier fashion, to form square-section uprights in serpentine curves to support bowed, padded arms. Again flutings were employed, on arm supports and on legs which finished in small turned feet. These chairs were most usually made of beech for they were invariably gilded.

Innumerable beechwood settees of the last quarter of the century were japanned black, picked out with flat gilt decoration, and the desire for variety was so strong in the 1770's and 1780's that mahogany was largely replaced by such light woods as satinwood for lavishly dainty drawing room chairs. Indigenous birch was tinted to form a cheaper substitute for legs, and chestnut was used for veneered effects.

George Hepplewhite appears to have come under the influence of painted decoration late in life, making greater use of mahogany with fine satinwood inlay. As Hepplewhite's name is so intimately associated with English chairs —perhaps the finest medium for his homely approach to furniture design—it is worth analyzing them in detail. But once again it must be emphasized that his *Guide*, published two years after his death, far from boasting of originality, specifically claimed to have followed "the latest or most prevailing fashions".

Compared with mid-century work, Hepplewhite chairs possess an air of grace just because they are constructed on a smaller scale, and this for no other reason than that Ince and Mayhew and their contemporaries had to contend with wide skirts and stiffened coats whereas Hepplewhite was at work while hoops were temporarily out of fashion.

Like Adam, Hepplewhite designed some chairs with rectangular backs reminiscent of the mid-century style, and even a few with vertical bars grouped to suggest the earlier splat form joining the seat-rail. But even these had their straight lines broken with tiny circles or rosettes carved in relief. Others took the French lyre shape. But the shapes now associated with Hepplewhite are the shield, upholstered or pierced and perhaps first introduced by Gillows of Lancaster where Hepplewhite was apprenticed; the heart shape and the oval, usually, but not invariably, concave. A few were round, the "wheel spokes" sometimes foliated and radiating from a small central "hub" painted or inlaid. Some painted satinwood chair-back settees also had the wheel shaping.

In each case the back was upheld entirely by the uprights, which were shaped continuations of the back legs. Within the oval or shield some variant of the pierced and carved splat supported the sitter's back. Its treatment was extremely varied. Hepplewhite, as chair-maker to the Prince of Wales, had a natural liking for the feathers motif, which sometimes formed the entire splat within the shield; he is also associated with the wheat-ear, and various long narrow leaf designs. The faces of the various pieces forming the chair back were often sunk or slightly moulded and low relief carving was introduced to a considerable extent. But, in direct contrast to Chippendale work, carving was now largely confined within the smoothly curving outline of the back. And on some uncarved examples even the basic construction of the back was concealed behind a bland facing of cross-banded veneer.

The arms of chairs of the so-called Hepplewhite period often rose from where the front legs joined the seat instead of being screwed to the side-rails. They then curved swiftly back and up in concave or serpentine line to horizontals which, for greater strength, were set rather high on the back uprights. This style was carried further in subsequent Sheraton designs. But while Sheraton showed a particular feeling for the association of arm and front leg—illustrated in detail in his books of designs—Hepplewhite gave a singular charm to the union of arm and back upright.

Hepplewhite seats were usually over-stuffed, finished with brass-headed nails. Among upholstery fabrics of the day were haircloths, coloured and figured, as well as silks. Seats on these chairs and six- or seven-feet-long settees were typically serpentine in outline. In contrast to mid-century designs the legs invariably tapered,and many were without stretchers. Often their square edges were relieved with beading; alternatively, slightly raised moulding on the arrises edged sunken panels delicately carved with diminishing pendant husks (Page 57, Fig. 82). These might end in plinth feet; other feet were carved in leaf forms, and some followed the Adam style of spade and thimble shapes.

Other chairs in the Hepplewhite style had turned legs, reeded or fluted, in the French-Adam manner. One popular carved device was a ribbon spiralling down each leg (Page 57, Fig. 83). On these chairs the arm supports were also turned.

Traces of the cabriole leg, very slender and only slightly curved, can be ascribed to as late as the 1770's; yet to Hepplewhite and Sheraton the term had already lost its meaning and was applied to types of chairs, perhaps confused with the cabriolet carriage then the rage. With similar naïveté Hepplewhite's *Guide* gave the low, broad bergère chair the outlandish name of barjier chair. The contemporary French "duchesse" has often been called a window-seat, but paintings of the time—by Zoffany for example—suggest less limited use.

Late in the period associated with Hepplewhite the tendency to produce ever lighter and lighter chairs prompted a return to more rectangular outlines. The cresting-rail, very thin towards the sides, often formed, or rode over, a narrow central panel slightly curved to fit the sitter's back and variously decorated. Below, there might be a vase-shaped splat or an array of narrow lattice bars rising from a cross-rail only a few inches above the seat. In some Hepplewhite work these bars were linked with carved loops suggesting drapery (Page 55, Fig. 64), then a popular treatment for mahogany chairs and a feature of Sheraton design.

In chair design Sheraton bridged the transition between the ever-refining elegance of the eighteenth century and the weighty solemnity of the nineteenth. The change is typified by the turned work of the period. Adam made but limited use of turning. Hepplewhite was responsible for a considerable number of finely proportioned designs, and early Sheraton examples brought such work to its climax. Yet by the 1820's it would appear that the whole essence of the craft had been lost. The earlier Sheraton designs were so light and delicate that they necessitated faultless material and workmanship.

The main developments in Sheraton chair design were this ever-greater use of turning and the re-emergence of more rectangular lines. Sheraton regarded turning as a fine art. In some chairs even the cresting rail was turned, the raking uprights scrolled to hold it. In very light chairs the back legs, too, were turned, and indeed Sheraton has been regarded as the best interpreter of the Louis XVI turned leg. But on the whole the underframing and leg construction of his chairs lacked the strength of the back and arm design.

His love of rectangular lines was given full play in chair and settee backs. Even when he adopted the Hepplewhite shield he gave it a straight line across the centre of the top. But the typical Sheraton back was the more or less square shape enclosed by the uprights, by the low cross-rail, and by the crest-rail which, however, was almost invariably modified to break the entirely straight line across the top used by Adam. Within this square, and unconnected with the seat-rail, Sheraton introduced a variety of fillings which, however, generally avoided the basic vertical splat form of earlier work. The nearest approach consisted of slender vase-, urn-, and lyre-shaped verticals. Delicate vertical and horizontal rails were often decorated with carving of drapery, bows, and the like. He recommended satinwood quite as much as mahogany, some picked out with gilt. Indeed, by early in the nineteenth century mahogany was chiefly a parlour and bedroom wood; rosewood, tulipwood, and zebrawood being typical choices for the drawing room.

In addition to his care for outline, Sheraton delighted in much surface decoration. This especially included inlay—husk, fan, oval, sunburst, and fine lines of stringing. On satinwood he recommended either inlay or paint. His painted motifs were more naturalistic and floral than those of Adam; a characteristic was their application to the bare wood.

A typical basis for more ambitious painting in the Italian style was the back of a chair on Adam lines, in which a rectangular panel, slightly curved and often with a considerable backward rake, formed the central section of a turned or twisted back rail. A graceful treatment consisted of four or five narrow horizontal reeded bars, between plain reeded uprights, supporting the panel. A lower cross-rail, consisting of a second, smaller group of horizontal bars, then supported a smaller panel. This panel form was developed until a wholly rectangular cresting-rail was enclosed between simply turned uprights. When the style was taken to its logical conclusion, as in earlier oak and walnut work, the wide rectangular cresting rail was made to ride over the tops of the back uprights, fitting on to them with tapering dovetails (Page 55, Fig. 66).

Hepplewhite chair-back construction placed little dependence upon a cross-rail above the seat. In Sheraton design this was an important feature, frequently semi-circular and inlaid or carved. Arms on Sheraton chairs followed some of the Hepplewhite designs, sweeping up to join the back uprights at a steep angle near their tops. From the side, most were seen to be S-shaped; on plan they were serpentine and most often rose from extensions of the front legs. Later examples might be reeded and Sheraton styles of the nineteenth century included elaborate arm ends with winged caryatides, dolphins, eagles' heads. Chair seats might be rectangular, oval or with some more elaborate front shaping, befitting drawing room chairs intended to be finished in japanning and touches of gilt. Front legs were most usually taper-turned and moulded. Dining chairs, which Sheraton himself recommended in his *Dictionary* (1803) should be "respectable and substantial-looking chairs", had rectangular back legs, parallel and curving well back. He suggested various forms of stretcher but most of his late mahogany designs were free of them.

In legs too, however, Sheraton's style became less and less happy as he strove to keep in fashion. In particular the japanned and painted furniture of this period often showed legs splaying out at the bottom, without feet (Page 57, Fig. 84). Many of these little beechwood chairs, caned on seat and on oval or rectangular back, showed decoration suggestive of contemporary coach painting.

Sheraton regarded painted chairs as suitable for a breakfast or tea room, but even some of his drawing room mahogany designs might be picked out with gilt in the French manner. Upholstery was dominated by the horse-hair that was also used extensively on the early nineteenth century settee—that scroll-headed, straight-backed affair mounted on curved and splayed-out legs fitted with castors.

Sheraton's Empire designs did no more than reflect the current vogue for reproducing the actual furniture of the ancient Romans, Greeks and Egyptians. This period was marked, indeed, by the great diversity of its chair styles, ancient, rococo and Gothic; but typical work might show scrolled-over cresting and either turned or flat curved cross-rails, the turning often showing rope-twist treatment, and the flat rails inlay or the brass mounts that caught

Sheraton's fancy. Brass line and scroll ornament on rosewood or mahogany was a feature of this period. Arms on such chairs, if any, might be straight, their ends scrolling over their fluted or reeded concave supports. A less satisfactory design was the S curving roundly down to meet the seat with a little scroll. Below the dipping caned and cushioned seat—dipping at the sides in some Empire work—the front legs swept forward in a concave curve; they showed pateræ at seat level and were taper-turned or reeded. The back legs followed similar sweeping lines to the rear. None of this, however, could compare with some of Sheraton's more extravagant designs, such as his Nelson chairs with their dolphins and anchors, his Herculaneums with their splaying legs and Roman ornament, and such Egyptian curiosities as one in which two carved camels formed the back.

7

COUNTRY CHAIRS

WHEN Charles II came to the throne in 1660 only London and four other towns had more than 10,000 inhabitants and few contemporary maps attempted to mark such straggling roads as connected them. Obviously, then, most everyday furniture was of local, country make, new fashions travelling but slowly and every small craftsman adapting them as best he could to the oak, ash, beech or elm wood that happened to be to hand.

It has been pointed out that during the Cromwellian years special impetus was given to these country workers, resulting in such elaborate designs as the "Yorkshire" and "Derbyshire" chairs. Other localities clung more nearly to the fashions set by London: for example, on the high-backed "Lancashire" chair simply-pierced, shaped cresting often topped the heavy square panelling that filled the upper half of the tall back, and the panelling might be incised or even heavily carved. But the uprights were given local individuality with squat, pointed finials. Moreover, the front legs, with their alternating square and round turned portions, linked by a heavily turned front stretcher, often resembled exactly those of the Yorkshire-Derbyshire types.

These various oak chairs were obviously still regarded as important pieces of furniture, deserving lavish treatment. They were country-made but belonged in type, if not always in actuality, to the years which preceded the Restoration mood. Thereafter, ornament began to supersede function: fashion demanded furniture for no purpose beyond elegant adornment of spacious apartments. For the first time, then, there was distinct contrast and not merely a difference of degree between the furniture of fashion and the indigenous country product.

Country chairs designed to replace rough-hewn stools and benches in farmhouse and cottage took various shapes, two features marking their evolution—the use of variously combined but wholly local timber and the application of mass-production methods. The result was in each case a product cheap enough to develop wide new markets throughout most of the eighteenth century.

Of these chairs the best known are the Windsor and the less individualistic ladder-back and spindle-back, all of which showed considerable similarity of construction. All broke away from the well-established chair construction methods based upon rectangular mortise-and-tenon joints.

The Windsor, indeed, was completely a departure from earlier chair designs—in its shaped saddle seat, in its round taper-tenon joints, in the disassociation of legs from back and arms, in the use of bent wood in back, arms and stretchers. Many explanations of its name have been suggested. The most probable is that it was associated with the ancestors of the Earls of Plymouth, whose family name was Windsor, of Bradenham in Buckinghamshire, the county most famous for these chairs.

The material for these various country chairs consisted of timber grown in the localities where they were produced. In the majority of Windsors several kinds of wood were introduced, each to meet specific constructional requirements. Tough elm was used for the seat, straight-grained beech for the legs, lissom fruit-woods, birch and especially yew for the bent work. Manufacture required only simple tools, of which one of the most important was the primitive pole lathe used from Tudor times. Thus, the component parts of the chair could largely be shaped in bulk where the wood was felled, and simply assembled at so little cost that Windsors were long the chairs of the royal parks, and ladder-backs typical of coffee house and inn.

The Windsor went through a variety of distinct phases but it is impossible to ascribe any exact dates. Old types lingered on and mid-nineteenth-century catalogues illustrated many remarkably similar to those of perhaps 120 years earlier.

This chair appears to have originated in Berkshire and more especially Buckinghamshire, where elms abound in the rich valleys and beech and fruit-woods and majestic yew drive deep roots into the grey chalk of the downs. In these woods the "bodgers" set up their little tents, each with its pole lathe. This consisted of a pliant lath fixed to the tent roof and combined with a foot treadle to pull on the ends of a cord fixed around the work, thus revolving the wood under the worker's chisel.

From the Wycombe area the Windsor chair design spread to Devon and to Somerset, where it was known as the stick-back. By the end of the eighteenth and early in the nineteenth century various stick-backs were common throughout the Midlands. Even in Lancashire a solid, handsome type was being produced, usually made entirely in that mahogany of the Windsor chair, yew wood. It seems probable that the earliest Windsors date from the beginning of the eighteenth century, although one reference suggesting manufacture prior to 1708 has been cited in America.

The most direct predecessor to the Windsor was the old three-legged milking stool: Italians were adding low spindle backs to their stick-leg stools by the end of the fifteenth century. This stool was the humblest possible piece of furniture: the superior, rectangular stool with mortise-and-tenon joints was specifically distinguished from it by the name "joined stool". Like the milking stool, the Windsor had as its basic feature a solid block of thoroughly seasoned elm (sometimes ash). Into this four holes were drilled with a bit so that turned legs, tapered at the top, could be heated and driven into it; these swelled, to fit more tightly, as they cooled. In some chairs the tops of the legs came right through the seats.

This seat was given an entirely new comfort by its characteristic shaping—hollowed out with an adze and finished with a bow-shaped spoke-shave. Like the stool, the earliest legs were plainly turned, their outward splay unchecked by stretchers. Early ornamental turning consisted of no more than a little shaping towards the ground, in contrast to later and more elaborate leg turnery. Above the seat, the back was made up of perhaps nine or ten plain-turned vertical spindles supporting the slightly curved crest-rail. In early work the top edge of this crest was shaped like a comb; an occasional rarity has been found with a typical late Stuart crown carved upon it. By the nineteenth century, crests had lost their shaping, and thus comb-back Windsors the meaning of their name, in the typical Regency rail.

American Windsors with their very splayed legs confined themselves to plain spindle-backs, like the earliest English examples, but in both the comb-back and the later hoop-back made in this country a splat was frequently introduced down the middle, flanked by three or four spindles on each side. Early splats were plain, in the Queen Anne fiddle and vase shapes; only later came the various pierced decorations, in the wake of richer chair fashions. Another early development sometimes found on the comb-back was the addition of two strengthening spindles forming a V from the crest down to a tail-piece extension at the back of the chair seat.

The idea of introducing bent wood appears first to have been adopted in the horizontal hoop which formed a full half-circle across the back and out to the front of the chair as the arm horizontals, following the outline of the seat. The back spindles passed right through this hoop and some four more spindles each side supported the arm with similar taper-tenon joints. Only in such later varieties as the Lancashire Windsor was this arrangement modified. The back spindles then ended in the arm hoop, half-way down the back. Below this, the back and arm supports consisted of some half-dozen stouter, turned balusters resembling the heavily-turned legs and stretchers.

Once shaped wood came into use it was no great advance to replace the comb crest-rail with the characteristic hoop, consisting of a single bar of rectangular section raking well backwards and forming the entire frame of the chair back. On the single "low-back" chair the taper-turned ends of this pliant bar were bedded in the seat; on the armed, "high-back" variety it arose from the horizontal hoop already described. When arms were fitted to a low-back, they joined the back hoop at about half height. In some chairs the end supports to the arms were differentiated from the other narrow spindles, thickened and given pronounced forward and outward curves. Yew is peculiarly difficult to work, very hard yet brittle, and the bow of the back had to be steamed with the bark retained on one side and removed from the other, then levered into shape and cooled in a clamp.

Inevitably the cabriole shape was soon adopted for the front legs of many Windsors; the earliest hoop backs date from this period although few designers found any satisfactory line for the union of curving leg and block seat. Moreover, few makers dared abandon the use of turned stretchers and these greatly detracted from the grace of their products. From about the mid-century even the front stretcher might be of bent wood: this was called the crinoline or cow's horn line. It approximated to the arrangement of straight stretchers in which two from front to back were joined by a third across the middle of the chair, for the front stretcher curved well back under the middle of the chair, to be met by two short straight ones slanting inwards from the back legs.

Pad feet were usual; hoof feet, associated with early cabriole legs, were occasionally used and stood up well to the rough wear that has conspicuously reduced the height of many an old Windsor with the later type of turned and somewhat tapering leg. The line of the later baluster, on both front and back legs, consisted typically of a slight broadening from the point of insertion at the seat down to a ball or bobbin turning at knee height; then a slow swell to contain the taper-tenon of the stretcher followed by a slow taper to a smaller ankle-height ball or ring and a final taper to the ground without foot shaping (Page 57, Fig. 86).

So much for the general outlines of the Windsor. In each detail, throughout the century, its quality depended entirely upon the prowess of individual craftsmen, and crude workmanship is no assurance of age. Occasionally a craftsman strove to make it a fashion chair. A few were made of mahogany, with no bent members. Some seats were shaped to perfection. Some backs were given quite elaborate

"Gothic" forms, varying from a few interlacing arches in place of the vertical spindles to a trio of finely pierced "Gothic" splats. Even the hoop back might become a "Gothic" arch, ill-suited to the extravagantly deep-shaped cabriole legs. "All sorts of Yew tree, Gothic and Windsor chairs" were advertised by William Webb of Newington, Surrey, as late as 1785.

Many splats suggest other fashions of the second quarter of the century and probably date from 1750 onwards; it must have been almost the end of the century before Windsors appeared with the "Hepplewhite" wheel splat, pierced with a circle or ellipse filled with six or eight spokes or with a rough outline of the Prince-of-Wales feathers. A reflection of Sheraton's times was the pierced fan splat. As with fashion chairs, a few Windsor settees were designed in the two-chair or three-chair style.

American Windsors were often painted. The English way was generally to leave them plain—not even polished—so that house-proud cottagers could keep them clean by scouring with sand. Some, however, were stained or painted black.

While the Windsor type dominated Buckinghamshire, other regions were developing their own country styles. There was the Norfolk chair, for instance, with a similar saddle seat, and an elaborate back of splats and vertical spindles between curved crest and cross-rails, sometimes decorated with small balls (Fig. 104). The "Mendlesham" chair of Suffolk was another variant. Better known are the Lancashire spindle-back and the Yorkshire ladder-back in which, also, there was little call for the usual rectangular mortise-and-tenon joinery.

Fig. 104

These simple country chairs, developing late in the seventeenth century, were popular throughout most of the eighteenth and especially during the second half of it. Oak and walnut as well as ash, elm, and beech were used in their simple construction and many had rush seats—a material similarly appreciated by the Egyptians nearly six thousand

a. A rich example in ebony and silver of a table design extremely popular in post-Restoration England. The twist-turned legs, slightly tapering upwards, are mounted on flat, waved stretchers above the ball feet.

A mid-eighteenth-century mahogany rd table in which part of the side friezes ld concertina-fashion when the table is osed. Only the front legs are topped by unded frieze shapings, the back legs following the earlier style.

c. A mahogany "silver" table of about 1755-60 in which the fret-cut gallery and frieze follow an elaborate serpentine outline. Cluster-column legs on guttae feet.

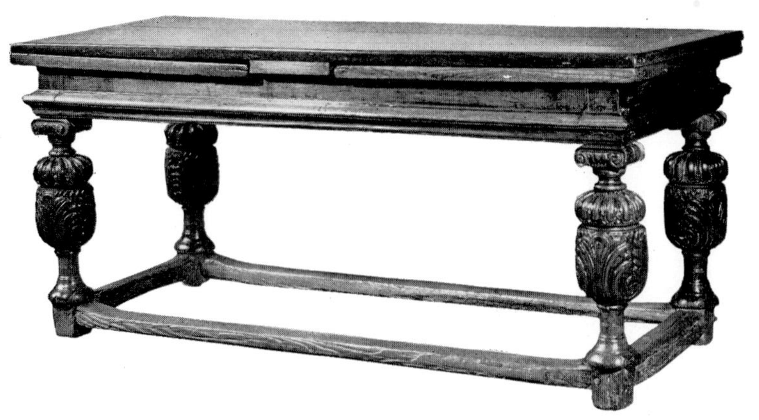

a. The earliest form of extending table was the Elizabethan oak draw-table. A the end may be discerned the bearers which project to support the additiona length of table drawn out from under the central portion at each end.

b. This pair of inlaid satin-wood side tables was designed to be placed togethe thus forming a circular central table when required. Typical details include th fan design on the centre top, and pendant husks down the tapering legs. About 178

c. Yet another method of varying the table's size is shown in this early-nineteent century pillar-and-claw table with two D-shaped additions. The method of linkir is clearly shown.

years ago. Their construction was simple. Turned back legs were prolonged above the seat to form the back uprights; between these was introduced a filling which consisted of either rows of vertical spindles let into the top and cross-rails, or a series of rectangular horizontal splats. Between perhaps 1725 and 1775 the front legs were turned with sturdy club or ball feet, but there was seldom wood to spare for curving cabriole knees (Page 57, Fig. 79). Between the front legs in early work there might be two turned stretchers, the upper with knobs or heavy bulges to the centre. There were two plain turned stretchers each side and one at the back. Later spindle-backs, like later ladder-backs, had only the one stretcher at the front and this lacked the pronounced bulge.

The principal interest in these homely little chairs, however, lies in the varied arrangements of the backs. Ladder-backs, associated with the Midlands, came originally from Holland, being known as Dutch chairs in the late seventeenth century. Between 1725 and 1825 they were also produced in great quantities in America under the name of slat-backs. Beech, ash and elm were usual woods and the slats were generally bent in slight curves to fit the sitter's back. Early examples had heavy, low backs with two, three, or four of these horizontal slats, but the later and more typical high, narrow back might enclose four or five, occasionally seven, slats, often in decreasing widths. The top rail might be straight but more often followed the curves of the cross-rails in such simple outlines as the cupid's bow and double-ogee curve.

The plainest ladder-back showed merely three plain rails, the finest most probably five in quite elaborate ribbon outline. The latter would be set off by legs and front stretcher turned in shapely swelling lines, but did not, of course, attempt to vie with the mahogany ladder-back of fashion with its finely pierced and carved slats.

The spindle-back often did show some slight attempt at carving, but little more than the early eighteenth century shell upon the top rail. Typically, this solid farmhouse chair had two rows of turned spindles in the back—five spindles to the row—armchairs having three rows. Rarer was the single row of spindles. Usually these slender spindles were turned in decorative silhouettes unknown in the rails of the Windsor. Early examples might show oval bulges in the cross-rails where the ends of the spindles were inserted, but the shaping disappeared before the middle of the century. A later trend, reflecting a mahogany fashion, was the use of a wide cresting-rail with ear-pieces extending well beyond the uprights.

The spindles themselves varied considerably in shape, long thin spindles being associated with North Lancashire, and thicker, bolder lines with the south of the county. Chairs with exceptionally tall backs containing two rows of long spindles were probably made in the Midlands after 1760; the rarer specimen with a single row of spindles, straight legs, and a wide seat, might come from Cumberland. On a rush-seated spindle-back, fillets of wood to hide the rough edges appear to have been an individual taste and cannot be taken as an aid to dating. Big grandfather arm-chairs, rockers, and baby chairs were also made.

As with the Windsor chair, an occasional George III spindle-back might be given a considerable air of distinction. Turning then played a less important part, frame, legs, and stretchers being of rectangular section. Simple piercing was attempted on the top-rail and the spindles were fine examples of the turner's craft. If these fail to prove wholly satisfying it is merely because the unelaborated rural product has the fundamental appeal of fitness for its purpose. The working sheepdog has no use for jackets and bows.

8

TABLES

IN feudal and early Tudor England the table was essentially the "board" on which mighty meals were served in the great hall of the manor. The food was prepared and dished up on crude side tables, often no more than slabs of wood mounted on three or four sticks, like the primitive milking stool. But the main dining table was a splendid affair, and even before 1600 had developed several distinct styles of construction.

The old manor hall was a general living room. Between meals tables were merely encumbrances, and the basic principle governing most early design was that they should fold into the minimum amount of space. The master and mistress and a few guests might eat at a "dormant" table on a dais at one end of the hall. At right angles to this, long narrow tables on folding trestles were so placed that the rest of the company could sit on forms along one side with their backs to the wall while being served from the front—two basic requirements for eating in comfort in those uneasy days. Old MSS. occasionally show tables horse-shoe-shaped, the diners facing the centre where the servants stood. But more usually the table was straight, the three or four heavy planks, four to six inches thick, that formed the top, of oak, elm, or fruit-wood, being secured by cross-bearers and mounted on two simple X-shaped trestles. Shovel-boards, Tudor forerunners of the billiard table, might be as long as forty feet, but some trestle tables were quite small. The rough finish was disguised by richly draped cloths: even the nondescript farmhouse had its "carpets" and napery for "cup-board" and table.

By the early sixteenth century, the supports, while still entirely separate, might each consist of a flat vertical board mounted on a massive foot so that each somewhat resembled a broad I, or alternatively of a square pillar on an X foot. The obvious development of this was the linking of the two uprights with a long central stretcher to give greater rigidity. This stretcher was tusk-tenoned through the upright trestles and its protruding ends secured with pegs for speedy dismantling (Fig. 105 shows end view of trestle; Fig. 106 detail of tusk tenon).

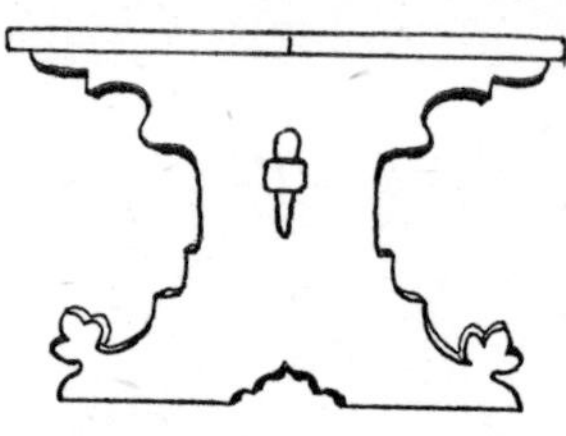

Fig. 105

These trestle constructions appear to have continued until after 1600. During the later years of the sixteenth century the two vertical supports, whether independent or stretcher-linked, reflected the fashion for bulbous cup-and-cover shapes characteristic of late Elizabethan days. But already, early in the sixteenth century, new types of table were becoming established. As early as 1526 Bishop Grosbeste was denouncing dining "in corners and secret places": heads of many households were beginning to enjoy the privacy of their own living rooms and in consequence a new elegance was being demanded of tables. The saving of space was no longer a primary consideration, although folding "joined tables" were devised for army camp life.

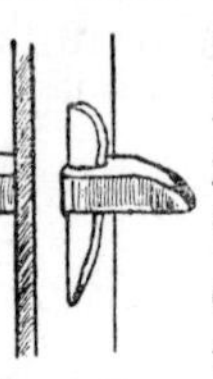

Fig. 106

Instead of two supports the early living room table had four or more turned legs held rigid by stretchers placed almost at floor level. The boards which formed the table top, cross-framed at each end, were dowelled to the underframing, this consisting of a broad frieze tenoned into the square tops of the legs. The stretchers either directly linked all the legs or consisted of two short bars across the ends linked by one running centrally down the length of the table. Stretchers early in the sixteenth century were often T-shaped in section, the broad flat top supporting the sitters' feet and, when not in use, the benches or stools; this shape was discontinued in the following century.

a. In this walnut writing-table the gate legs, recessed into the main framework, open outwards to hold the unfolded top. The inverted-cup legs date from about 1690 and this style of table continued into the eighteenth century.

b. A nest of tables in the Sheraton style, finely made of figured rosewood. About 1810.

c. A late-eighteenth-century Pembroke table, the figured satin-wood inlaid with ribbons, swags, and conch shells. The legs are mounted on roller castors.

a. A mid-seventeenth-century folding table in oak on the lines of the credence cupboard. The legs are plainly turned and there is low-relief carving on the frieze and drawer—a feature of some early gate-leg tables.

b. A post-Restoration gate-leg table with four gates. The shapely baluster-turned legs have ball-feet and the stretchers moulded edges.

Stools and benches at this period were constructed on very similar lines and often made to match the tables. The stools might be made to tilt forward slightly, their legs widely splayed, back and front, for greater rigidity. Forms often resembled long stools, but trestle types, with and without tusk-tenoned stretchers, were also produced.

The early living room table is often called a refectory table, but the term has no particular significance. Its decorative treatment followed the trends of its period, often featuring rich carving such as flowers and foliage or gadrooning on the frieze, resembling that on contemporary buffets, but being reduced to more formal incised line-work in the seventeenth century. Later Elizabethan work might show the frieze inlaid with fine black and white checker patterns on all sides; on side tables, otherwise similar, backs were left plain.

Accompanying legs had their massive cup-and-cover or melon swellings typically carved with gadrooning and jewel-shapes on the "cover" and acanthus leaf on the "cup". Some late-sixteenth-century legs were clumsy adaptations of classic columns, but such details as Ionic capitals were largely discontinued in the seventeenth century when carving generally decreased and legs displayed the more restrained contemporary turning such as the uncarved, oval swell ascribed to Dutch influence. Many had roundish feet below the rectangular blocks which housed the stretcher joints. After the Restoration, carved acanthus leaf corner brackets often linked legs and frieze, and on the frieze itself the Flemish style of glued-on bosses and split turnings was sometimes introduced, but proved less accommodating than flatly incised strapwork.

An important modification of this design was the contemporary draw-table—the earliest attempt to match the table to the number of diners. Even by the mid-sixteenth century it was largely taking the place of the plain refectory design. With similar legs and frieze, this table mounted a more elaborate underframing: the top was in three parts, the main portion completely covering two flap extensions which could be pulled out when required. These ends were so mounted on slanting bearers that whether one or both were drawn out the table top remained level.

For perhaps the first quarter of the seventeenth century the draw-table continued popular; before the mid-century the design had been largely out-moded by yet another space-saving notion—the gate-leg table. It is generally suggested that the earliest consisted of a table with three rigid legs and one gate-leg structure which, with the flap open, formed a round table. Half of one of the rigid legs swung out to support the flap.

Many different designs were evolved, some with as many as twenty legs and with tops square, rectangular, round, elliptical, and in the eight-sided "credence table" style, but the basic construction was the same and markedly solid and workmanlike in its mortise-and-tenon joints and dowelled top. Briefly, it consisted of a normal rectangular frame on four legs supporting the central immobile portion of the table. Let into this, most usually on each of the long sides, was a "gate-leg" constructed of two uprights linked by top and bottom stretchers, the inner upright pivoting on the main framing and the other swinging out to prop up the table flap. When closed, the gate-leg fitted neatly into the main table framing, in which the stretcher was halved to accommodate it.

In early work the top was most frequently round; square tops are associated with Dutch influence. In Charles I's reign the end supports of the main table framing followed the lines of the earlier vertical trestle boards on wide feet and were linked by a solid plank stretcher; soon after the mid-century designs also included turned baluster legs, sometimes cheapened to flat boards in baluster profile. These were mounted on trestle feet and linked by two narrow stretchers. Occasionally incised carving was introduced on the frieze ends of early work.

The eight-legged design, now most common, consisted of four turned stretcher-linked legs to support the main framing and two more legs on each side forming the gates. Even when the legs were elaborately turned the stretchers might be plain or slightly moulded. As on contemporary chairs, turning was omitted and solid square blocks left for all mortise-and-tenon joints. Early feet might be square; later most usually plain balls. Spanish feet were occasionally introduced in late seventeenth century examples. Often a drawer was inserted in the main framing, sliding on one central bar instead of side runners.

Oak was always the wood most associated with gate-leg tables although some were made in fruit-woods and walnut and later a few in mahogany. In later work there were certain advances in constructional detail, although country examples were usually far behind the times. Thus, seventeenth-century workmen experimented with various shapes for the meeting of the side flaps with the central portion of the top before the rule joint (Fig. 107) became established. This joint concealed the hinges and left no gap; often it gave the table a similar thumb or ovolo mould on all four edges of the central rigid portion: the flaps had this mould only on their exposed edges, the hinge edge having the complementary concave shaping to make a perfect union.

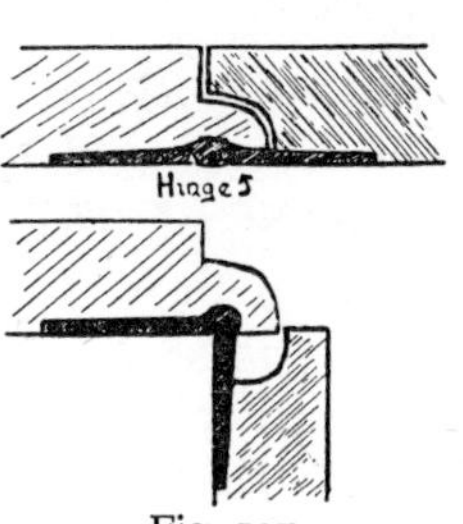

Fig. 107

Screws were a later seventeenth-century innovation, so that wrought iron hinges in early examples had to be fixed with nails; in the eighteenth century screws were also used to replace the earlier dowel pegs in fixing the top (from underneath), while glue replaced the pins in the mortise-and-tenon joints. Of necessity these tables were always sturdy structures, but on small examples where an earlier craftsman would introduce a noticeably thin top, a later one might achieve a similar effect by merely rounding off the lower edge of the top.

A variant of the gate-leg table had the gate legs on one side only, and when closed the flap—half the table top—did not hang down but folded back over the fixed portion. The legs were so hinged that they closed together at the back of what then served as a fashionable side table. Often both halves of the table top were hinged, the lower giving access to a well in the under-framing.

These were often very small tables, and the fact must not

be overlooked that from early in the seventeenth century much simpler little tables were also being made—miniature versions of the refectory type. At first they were mainly of oak, later of walnut, their legs following the various fashions for ball, twist and baluster turning. These must have served for games, writing and bedroom use, and were the forerunners of the dressing and writing tables dealt with later.

Indeed, even by the early years of the seventeenth century there was considerable variety among English tables. An inventory of 1624 refers to various round tables (old drawings show round as well as rectangular tables on the heavy baluster legs of Stuart days), "a standing table for tailors to work on", "a pair of white and black checkered tables", "a long standing table, with a longe forme and bench fastened in the ground". . . . But by the end of the century an entirely new standard of elegance had been attained in table construction: ornamental, "occasional" furniture was becoming established. Under such names as side, pier, and console tables, they played a conspicuous part in eighteenth-century furniture fashions.

For dining, several gate-leg tables were then generally used, plain fixed tables, elliptical, round, and rectangular, being ever-recurrent substitutes. In 1679 Ham House had eight cedarwood tables in the "Great Eating Room". Sometimes a rectangular gate-leg table was further extended by the addition of another small table at each end. At first, after the Restoration, oak gave place to much work in solid walnut, which showed to perfection in the finely proportioned twist-turned legs of the later seventeenth century. But the Continental insistence upon decoration soon found expression in more lavish new treatments for English tables too.

On the side table, now, not only the frieze and legs were decorated but often also the top. Well-balanced quarters of veneer and many extremely fine marquetry designs were introduced, matched on the frieze and handled with special care on such details as drawer fronts, although the frieze was seldom as deep as on contemporary dressing and writing tables and lacked their curving outlines. The top was bordered with bandings of cross-grain or herring-bone walnut, and cross-grain veneer was applied to the ovolo-moulded edge and to the flat stretchers. Japanning decorated some English tables, and some lacquered specimens were imported from the East. Before the end of the century, some tops and frames were covered in gilded gesso arabesque patterns, and richest of all were the massive tables of silver possessed by those of Charles II's favourites who could afford this sumptuous French fashion.

Towards the end of the century baluster leg shapings returned to favour on all types of tables as on chairs, but did not so thoroughly oust the Italian-inspired twist-turning. Some of the finest late twist-turned examples, like some stair balusters, rose from vase-turned bases and tapered slightly towards the top. On country work a suggestion of twist-turning was simply achieved with rectangular legs in closely waved profile.

The foreign influences that brought such variety to late seventeenth-century chair leg design similarly affected tables, and William's reign produced various trumpet and mushroom shapes, the pronounced swell at knee height being either round or many-sided. Some later baluster and double-baluster shapes were particularly graceful. Other minor tables were mounted on substantial S-scrolls, set at angles calculated to show to best advantage from close quarters. These legs were mounted on an arrangement of stretchers constructed as one separate unit dowelled on to the ball or bun feet.

On tables as on chairs, and on the various stands under chests of drawers, stretchers were important decorative features towards the close of the seventeenth century. On simple tables by the 1680's—even on some gate-legs of William's reign—they were beginning to be made plainly broad and flat, widening at the corners where they protruded squarely between turned legs and ball or bun feet (Fig. 108). Some ran directly from leg to leg, usually in deep concave curves which might be linked by a small

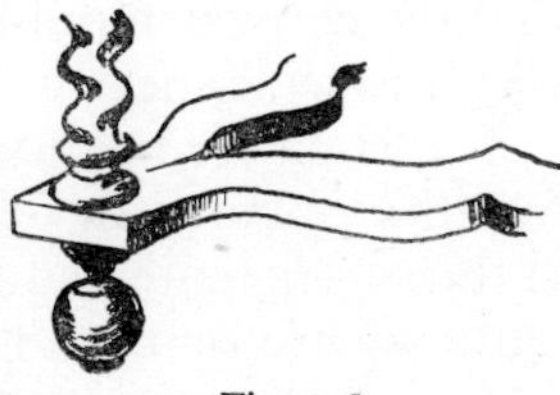

Fig. 108

circular shelf in the middle. But more often an X plan was used, or a modification of this form, the X interrupted and elongated at the centre by the small shelf. The plain X-shape was topped with a central finial; the shelf could be decorated with a movable ornament such as a piece of the newly-fashionable china. In all three designs the stretchers followed a waved outline throughout their length.

On tiny drawing room tables the stretchers might be as shapely and delicate as on costly Marot chairs. A small rectangular table, for instance, might have six legs, most richly carved, and swelling at knee and ankle height, with two sets of arching X stretchers topped by finials. These various designs had scarcely become established in this country, however, before the cabriole leg was introduced, near the turn of the century, and established an entirely new criterion of shapely grace.

The beginning of the eighteenth century was notable for its small walnut tables. Not only were they now used for dining, but most abundantly for those particular pleasures of the age, card playing and letter writing. The earliest English card tables were of the folding design already described, in which two gate legs on the straight side of a semi-circular side table swung out to receive the unfolded top. But when the late-seventeenth-century baluster turned legs were replaced by the slender cabrioles of the eighteenth, unfettered by stretchers, designers found a new freedom in planning extending tables.

For card playing, late in Anne's reign, was the rectangular table in which half the top unfolded to make a square. The customary piece of cloth, glued within a border of veneer and edged with braid or gimp, was thus concealed when not required for play. Some designs with three flaps opened to show either cloth-covered or veneered top. The vertical, slightly convex moulding around these tables contrasted with the wide, nearly flat ovolos of William's reign.

The simplest method of supporting the top when open was the obvious development of the construction shown in the seventeenth-century folding table already mentioned. On a square or rectangular table the whole of one of the four legs swung out, frequently complete with part of the table underframe. This gate-table construction was quite distinct from the earlier gate-leg table in which the mobile legs were additional to the main framing with the fixed legs and stretchers. In some other cases half the under-framing, complete with two of the four legs, could be drawn out to support the top. That part of the frieze was triple hinged on each side to fold in on itself when the table was closed.

The projecting corners of the square table top were rounded and slightly sunk to hold candlesticks, and the frieze, square on early work, soon followed a similar rounded outline until, shortly before the mid-century, the vogue for square-based candlesticks changed the fashion. Square projections at the table corners were then introduced; alternatively, pull-out trays were fitted to the splayed corners of the table. Sunken receptacles were usually provided to hold the players' money. These might be inlaid or cloth-lined, for these tables were essentially well-finished luxury articles.

By George I's reign these and other small tables for general use showed bolder, heavier cabriole legs, often finely carved. As designers developed the cabriole technique, the carving on knee and "shoulders" became more flowing while that on the knee itself reflected the passing vogues for lion masks, satyr masks, and acanthus and cabochon designs described in previous chapters.

Walnut long persisted as the most popular wood for occasional tables, and early mahogany work—in the straight-grained, heavy Santo Domingo wood—was developed on similar lines. But it must be remembered that every kind of plain country table was still being made in oak. At most their decoration consisted of the simplest walnut cross-banding. Many of these were for writing and bedroom use: it has been suggested that some tables mounted with solid tops instead of walnut veneers were intended to serve as wash-stands.

Most primitive tables of all were the cottagers' oak "cricket tables". The "cricket" was the companionable little stick-legged stool that, like its insect namesake, was associated with the warm welcome of the cottage hearth, and the table presumably took its name from this. Old manuscripts of the early fourteenth century depict such tables used for preparing and serving food, the splayed, stretcherless legs taper-tenoned into the solid wood of the top. The simplest were circular, with three square-cut tapering legs. Others were more elaborate, with stretchers; some had flap extensions. They were still being made in eighteenth-century workshops, especially in country districts of Hertfordshire, Bedfordshire, Cambridgeshire, and Essex.

Meanwhile, for the minority who could afford them, the same period was producing magnificent tables which were part of the architectural design of the early Georgian mansion rather than pieces of furniture. Accompanying tall mirrors and elegant candle-stands, they were designed to adorn such conspicuous features as the narrow piers of wall between the tall windows in important apartments. They were known variously as pier, side and console tables (console, French for bracket, distinguishing the table intended to be attached at the top to the wall and with the legs, bracket-fashion, curving into the base). Their framework consisted of ponderous groupings of S-scrolls, crouching eagles with arching wings, naturalistic carvings in soft woods in the Gibbons style, masks, scrolls, and foliage built up in gesso composition. Their borders and friezes were enriched with gadrooning, egg-and-dart (Fig. 109 shows two examples), Vitruvian scroll, key pattern, and similar classic touches. All were brilliantly gilded and all in the architectural traditions of Kent, Gibbs, Vanbrugh, and their contemporaries.

Fig. 109

The obvious reason for such treatment was the new fashion for huge mirrors in England. As wall decorations these were well within the architect's province: the tables associated with them were of necessity similarly treated. In particular, on both mirrors and tables, Continental fashions ordained the lavish use of gilding, whether the base were soft wood carving, gesso, or even carved

typical gate-leg with all
ers twist-turned in the post-
:ation manner. The joint
en the centre table top and the
flaps is square-cut.

b. In contrast this mid-eighteenth-century mahogany table demonstrates the simpler gate design. Typical details include ball-and-claw feet on plainly tapering legs, and rule joints to the flaps.

c. A notable gate table with a suggestion of cabriole shaping to the legs, carved knees, and ball-and-claw feet. The flaps show an unusual variant of the rule joint, harmonising with the scrolling lines of the legs.

a. A marble-topped side table realistically carved with early Georgian lion masks and lion paw feet. The frieze is carved in Vitruvian scrolls and its central motif suggests the French cabochon-and-leaf design.

b. The return to straight lines and low relief decoration which marked the second half of the eighteenth century is emphasized by this contrasting side table in the Adam style.

mahogany. Some of these tables were made with tops of marble or of the imitative composition scagliola which might incorporate chips of native stone such as Derbyshire marble. Houghton, in Norfolk, built for Robert Walpole in 1722-35, had a table of lapis lazuli accompanied by massive silver sconces.

Chippendale's *Director* (1754) illustrated a number of what he called "frames for tables", usually intended to carry marble slabs. The supports might consist of "two piping Fauns, leaning against two vines . . . neatly gilt", or "a Doric Entablature, with its Triglyphs and Metopes, supported by two Cariatides"—interesting as indicative of the kind of classic lore expected of a furniture designer in the mid-eighteenth century. Simpler early Georgian slabs were mounted on strongly carved cabriole legs, often displaying the shell motif in the centre of the frieze. The finely figured mahogany that became more generally available in the second half of the century contributed to some decline in the use of marble.

As mahogany became established there was a tendency towards lighter treatments and less exuberant gilding. The dense grain of the wood gave structural security to the extraordinarily delicate carving appropriate to the French modes adopted towards the mid-century. But it was not until the 1760's that the wealth of rococo decoration was displaced by the reticent grace of straight lines, low relief carving, and perfect proportions associated with Robert Adam.

By the mid-century the various early Georgian table designs had become well established, and spurred the leaders of furniture fashions to devise new and ever-more-charming tables to express the niceties of this society-minded era. For dining, fashion had returned, by the 1730's, to single and double extending tables. In these, the freedom from stretcher restriction allowed the full development of the gate principle. Frequently two of the four legs pivoted on wooden hinges built into the underframe. Further extensions might be achieved by fixing semi-circular tables to the ends of the flaps. These would do duty as separate pier or side tables at other times.

In early mahogany work each section of the table top consisted of a single piece of wood from the giant trees of Santo Domingo, this being one of the major uses for mahogany until the more richly figured varieties were introduced. The weight of such a table is remarkable. On handsome work carved cabriole legs might end in ball-and-claw feet. The legs on simple work were usually entirely plain-turned with no vestige of the cabriole knee and tapered only slightly to pad feet. A bill of the firm Bell & Moore dated 1734 priced "a Mahogany Dineing Table & frame boath flaps to fall down very good wood" at three guineas.

The diversity of tripod or "pillar-and-claw" tables necessitates a separate chapter. But Chippendale, Ince and Mayhew and many others were quick to appreciate a market for an infinite variety of other little tea and breakfast tables and galleried structures for displaying china. Here were unlimited opportunities for exploiting the fret-cut, card-cut, and trellis styles of the mid-century Chinese craze. The top of such a little table was of solid or veneered mahogany, rectangular or serpentine and, as with Chinese chairs, the frieze was elaborately fretted or card-cut and often linked by fretted brackets to the entirely straight, untapering legs. Each leg was often L-shaped in section, carved and pierced and if necessary reinforced with a central pillar inside the angle, rising from a solid plinth. Other legs were five-sided, on guttæ feet. Stretchers were occasionally reintroduced, arranged diagonally and similarly pierced.

The preparation of the mahogany, in any case little given to warping, and in good work built up of several layers, like modern plywood, ensured great strength even to extravagantly pierced designs. Painted or japanned work often emphasized the fretted detail by the use of contrasting colour on the returns. Another form of table leg consisted of a group of slender columns designed to suggest bamboo.

Similar designs were employed for more heavily built side tables. Legs on these could be treated more elaborately: there might be two at each front corner, linked together at the top and near the feet with Chinese, Gothic or French motifs. Some Chippendale breakfast tables had frieze drawers and shelving below their tops; brass wire work might enclose the shelf instead of wooden fret.

These breakfast tables were a feature of the period, result of a new social habit. Despite the ridicule of contemporary satirists, people of fashion were now rising late and breakfasting in their bedrooms, alone or with a chance visitor, on decorative little tables often mounted on leather castors. Chippendale, Hepplewhite, Sheraton, and George Smith all recorded this leisurely fashion. Smith, whose *Household Furniture* was first issued in 1808, recommended tables painted to match the breakfast china.

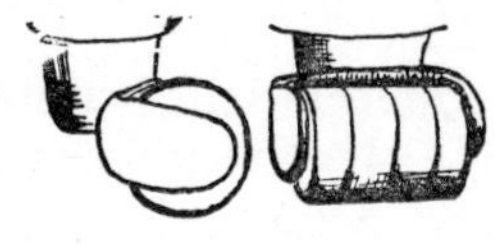

Fig. 110

Castors with broad leather rollers (Fig. 110) had been in use since the 1720's but by the 1770's several varieties of brass rollers were coming into vogue. Some were attached by means of tapering sockets in round or square section (Fig. 111); others, known as the peg-and-plate type (Fig. 112) were screwed to the bottom surfaces of the legs. These should be compared with the narrow, taller "wheel" castors (Fig. 113) dating from the end of the eighteenth century.

Fig. 111

Mention has already been made of the two-purpose card and tea tables with three flaps so arranged that they could be opened to offer a cloth-covered surface for cards or a brilliantly polished wooden top for the tea equipage. Some also served for writing, topped with green morocco leather; some were fitted for chess and backgammon. The simple card table at this time was plainly square, the top folding to a rectangle over a deep frieze, often fitted with drawers and mounted on legs plainly square except for a slight ovolo mould on their outer faces.

Fig. 112

Particularly appropriate for the fretted Chinese mode were the little tables for china display with vertical galleries an inch or so high around their rims, in vogue 1750-65. These suggested movable trays and indeed some tops were designed as such. These tables were

Fig. 113

planned to give a graceful informality to any part of a room—during an age of billowing skirts when there was considerable prejudice against any departure from the stylised arrangement of furniture around the walls.

Such fanciful designs, however, were essentially ephemeral. By the 1760's the French, the Chinese, and the Gothic, their bewildering details never entirely differentiated, were alike forgotten in favour of the classic calm sponsored by Robert Adam. For tables the change was particularly welcome, the new design wholly admirable. Finest of all, perhaps, were some of the "Adam" dining tables. The Victoria and Albert Museum shows a pair in which each has a fifth leg swinging out to support a deep flap. The end edges of these flaps are plainly square-cut: placed end to end they offer a combined table over seven feet long with four legs at the corners, four intermediate side legs and two under the centre. Plain vertical fluting graces the frieze which projects at the corners in low relief pateræ above the fluted legs. There is a frieze drawer at each end lined with blue paper. The table top has projecting splayed corners following the frieze outline, the figured veneers—in place of the earlier solid mahogany—bordered in a checker pattern of dark and light woods. This period delighted in the display of woods with particularly lovely figure and the finest inlays, catering for those households in which the low-hanging cloth was removed before dessert. The corresponding treatment of accompanying side tables is described in Chapter 11.

This arrangement of two extending tables was but one answer to the problem of matching the table to varying numbers of diners. Such craftsmen as Hepplewhite approved of dining tables provided by the set, and in 1771 Chippendale supplied David Garrick with "a set of mahogany dining-tables with circular ends to joyn together complete". These dining tables were expensive items. Some idea of the actual wholesale costs may be obtained from Shearer's *London Book of Prices* (1788). For making "a horse-shoe dining table, 7 feet long, 2 feet 6 inches wide", Shearer quoted £25, "the flap supported either way, plain taper legs, and an astragal round the bottom of the rail". Oiling and polishing would add another two shillings to the cost; even the hand-made blue paper lining a drawer would cost another three-halfpence.

In the late years of the century many patents were taken out for extending tables: usually the under-framing could be pulled out and loose leaves inserted. Ingenious scissor-action under-framing with numerous hinges was devised about 1800, at a time when heavy turning was tending to take the place of the squarely tapering leg with low relief carving.

By then, even dining tables were reflecting the popularity of the pillar-and-claw construction of tripod furniture. These tables were massive affairs, although the top could sometimes be lifted off the column for storage. The heavy central pillar was left square at the top to take the table framing above heavy turning and was mounted on a square plinth supported by four out-jutting "claw" feet. Some designs had the claws dovetailed into the plain base of the pillar itself. As with other tripod furniture the tendency at this period was for these claws to take a concave curve, although some were serpentine. Brass castors formed an integral part of typical designs: these had horizontal sockets (Fig. 114) and often took the popular lion-paw shape (Fig. 115). A large dining room might use two such tables and Sheraton planned tables built of these pillar-and-claw parts with a loose flap between each.

Fig. 114

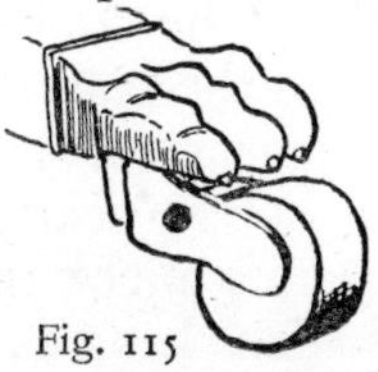

Fig. 115

Sheraton claimed a new design that had a circular top on a claw base and a large central dumb waiter. Many early nineteenth-century dining rooms had circular tables: Jane Austen's "Emma" introduced the innovation to Hartfield. D-shaping for table ends had an end-of-century vogue. Groups of pillars on a plinth came slightly later than the single column.

In contrast, tables such as Sheraton's "universal table", intended to serve for dining, went right back to the

Elizabethan draw-table principle, mounted on four plain tapering legs.

It was in pier, side, and other occasional tables, especially for the drawing room, however, that the late eighteenth century excelled. These were made in shapes innumerable, their tops circular and semi-circular, square, rectangular, and in a variety of serpentine outlines, their tapering legs turned, square-cut, or occasionally in very slender cabriole form, mounted on dainty scrolls. Their infrequent stretchers were planned in well-balanced curves, perhaps leading the eye to some central motif. The vertical parts of such tables were often straight or spiral fluted, carved in low relief, decorated with applied pateræ and similar classical detail or delicately painted.

On their tops these tables were more lavishly ornamented. Satinwood was the material *par excellence* as a basis for classic ornament—husks, swags, vases, attenuated scroll-work in the Pompeiian manner, and those "trophies" that Gibbons and his followers had carved so profusely for an earlier generation. The solid wood was enriched with delicate inlay; the carefully-matched veneer quarterings introduced panels of fine marquetry.

Quality variation was considerable, however, and may be judged by such inlay or marquetry motifs as the conch shell, as typical of the late eighteenth century as the scallop was of the century's early years. This might consist of any number of separate fragments, from five or six to nearly twenty. The finest work introduced a separate piece of wood for every variation of colour and shade. Less expensive results were achieved in a manner practised by makers of those special marquetry patterns known as Tunbridge ware, the light wood, such as holly, being shaded by scorching in hot sand.

By the 1780's, painted decoration was being used considerably on tables. Angelica Kauffmann, Cipriani, Pergolesi, and others produced notable designs incorporating pictorial panels in an Italianesque architectural style. But after about 1785 there was a more general vogue for the less expensive type of painted decoration, French-inspired and dominated by be-ribboned flowers and foliage. And on many table tops throughout the last thirty years of the century the treatment was altogether more formal, whether of inlay, marquetry, or superficial decoration. This consisted of a conventional border and a central panel, usually elliptical, containing a stylised fan or flower shape. Similar designs were applied to butler's trays—those large, galleried trays which, when placed on folding trestles, could serve as additional side tables. All these types of decoration—pictorial panels, flowers, and stylised fan shapes—might be combined on a single table top. The usual ground colours in painted work were straw, saffron, pale yellow, cream, pale green, and light puce, to tone with the walls of the room. Lacquer work was occasionally imitated on tables painted black or scarlet and enriched with gilt.

Sheraton devised some pier tables with marble tops, light in design and inevitably "elegant". But he appeared to prefer a top of satinwood bordered with double strips of cross-bandings separated by the rich "japanning" of the period. All this would be mounted on a frame of gilt or white and gilt, the legs carved in harmony with the flat decoration. He designed many ornamental legs for pier tables, in round and square section, carved and gilded or inlaid with panels and lines of stringing. He approved the re-introduction of stretchers which could support a vase or basket of flowers, set off by the pier glass behind.

Folding card tables followed the fashion with satinwood, inlaid or painted, on the closed top. This was now typically a semi-circle opening to a full circle for play, although such designers as Sheraton offered various alternative shapes, and before the end of the century straight-sided tables with rounded corners were in again. Although the turn of the century and the subsequent Regency period were marked by a love of rich veneers often edged with ebony stringing, workmanship was already tending to deteriorate, and Sheraton reflected contemporary ideas when suggesting how to produce the tops of "dry deal or faulty mahogany" to convey the impression of solid mahogany.

Tables of the Pembroke type were made as early as the 1760's but are particularly associated with Sheraton's work. When open, the two small falling flaps rested on fly brackets, most usually forming a top slightly squarer than a true ellipse. Often two drawers were introduced at one end of the central portion and imitation fronts the other. Shearer priced extra sham drawers on a small piece of furniture at fourpence each. Fluted legs in classic style gradually gave place to turned work, and some of Sheraton's Pembroke designs, like some of his other sofa tables, were mounted on "horse" legs. These were modifications of the ancient vertical trestles in which the two end uprights each rested on two out-jutting feet, most usually in concave curves above brassy castors. This style was also applied to cradles and to the "horse" or "cheval" glasses of the period.

Other Sheraton designs included a screen table for working in front of the fire and a pouch table for needlework, for which he suggested the fashionable black rosewood with brass frets. His "Harlequin" table was so called because "in exhibitions of that sort there is generally a great deal of machinery introduced in the scenery". This contained elaborate devices for raising writing table fitments out of the central well of what was, when closed, a flat breakfast table. Particularly charming were his little quartetto tables. These were usually designed in sets of four, slightly graduated in size to "nest" together in a style that has yet to be bettered.

a. This elaborate bed suggests Continental influence. The panelled headpiece has pilasters carved in human form in Elizabethan dress, and the pictorial motifs in the arches are reminiscent of "Nonsuch" chests. Beginning of the seventeenth century.

b. Left and right: oak box cradles made before and after the introduction of the hinged hood and side pieces during the seventeenth century. Centre: a spindle cradle of mahogany dating to the 1780's.

A tall, extremely handsome four-poster of the early eighteenth century at Hardwick Hall. The tester and elaborately shaped cornice are covered with cut velvet to match the curtains, and the ornate shell motif topping the bed-head is similarly decorated.

9

BEDS AND CRADLES

ONE of King Henry VIII's beds measured almost three yards square. Cardinal Wolsey owned beds at Hampton Court Palace to a total of some two hundred and eighty—gorgeous affairs of silken drapery. Throughout succeeding centuries, the best bed continued to be regarded as the householder's most prized piece of display furniture, and many an old inventory gives bedsteads and bedding pride of place in the principal dining and living rooms. Even in the eighteenth century stately beds with eighteen-foot pillars and tufts of nodding plumes formed an accepted background to the reception of favoured guests. Consequently, in society England, the story of even this basic piece of furniture is one of ever-increasing grandeur as succeeding generations lavished attention alternately upon its fabric hangings and its wooden frame.

People of lesser means had perforce to concentrate on comfort rather than such elegant display. Even King Henry III himself might have recourse to substitutes: for the great chamber at "Guildford" he ordered "on the blank wall at the head of our bed, to have painted the resemblance of a curtain or hanging. . . ." As for the scullion in the mansion attic, he was long resigned to the prickings of a primitive straw pallet. But not until the nineteenth century did the various massive structures we have come to know as four-posters cease to dominate English bed design.

Canvas pallets or mats must have served as peasant beds from time immemorial; they were easily laid upon chests or in the most primitive of box-like truckle bed-frames above the rushed floor, in an age when living and sleeping apartments were as yet not differentiated. Even in Tudor days wealthy travellers customarily took their "beds" with them—great bags of feathers, canvas sheets, blankets, coverlets of fur, which were given character and dignity by the rich curtains draped around them to provide both warmth and privacy. Indeed, in the early records of beds the wooden box framework appears to have been a minor consideration. Ceilings were still low and the fine hangings were suspended on iron rods or on cords which allowed them to be looped up out of the way during the day. By the 1580's Harrison, in his *Description of Britain*, was noting with dismay that even country farmers "have learnt to garnish their joined beds with tapestry and silk hangings."

Among the leaders of fashion in sixteenth-century England, however, the wooden framework was taking on a new importance. Mid-century inventories often refer to standing or joined bedsteads, some with settles attached at the foot. In these the open rectangular framework of oak was pierced and grooved along the side and end beams so that cords could be woven in and out to support the mattress, a method of construction also found on old settles. In the seventeenth century laths slotted into the framework sometimes served instead of cords and this became more general in the eighteenth century.

At the head of the bed panelling some four feet high protected the sleeper from draughts; at the foot there might be a corresponding panel or short corner posts, most usually turned. This was the basic structure, and in a lesser home the only ornament would be corner knobs to the plain panels. But the pride of the Elizabethan and early Stuart nobility was the superstructure which transformed such a stump bed into the most magnificent piece of furniture known even in those flamboyant days.

Where there had previously been no more than a wealth of drapery there might now be a weighty wooden structure. At the head of the bed the panelling was perhaps seven or eight feet high. At the foot, there might be similar panelling or more frequently two tall posts, often independent of the low, panelled end of the bed itself. And between them the high panelling and posts supported a huge wooden canopy extending over the whole area of the bed. It is obvious that this was but a development of the practice—still seen in parts of Brittany for instance—of tucking a bed into a panelled corner or alcove of a room. Its importance can be judged from the fact that the basic design persisted for nearly three centuries.

These Elizabethan beds are associated with particularly exuberant carving. Goddesses and wild men might be featured on the panel stiles between arcading and elaborate flower motifs. Border patterns included rows of semi-circles and various leaf forms. Some bed heads and ends were inlaid with coloured woods, and in 1609-10 the Earl of Salisbury paid £33 "for the gilldinge and workeing of one grete Bedsted with flowers birdes and personages annswerablle to the furneture thereof".

Carving changed in character as the period advanced, deep-cut uninhibited work giving place to more formal incised design and the typical "late oak" mitre-work and heavy panels of the mid-seventeenth century. Hiding places for jewellery abounded, as close as possible to the sleeper's head; cupboards were introduced and even cupboard shrines.

The massive oak columns at the foot of the bed, on heavy square bases, were similarly typical of their age. Some of the earliest were slender and delicately carved (Fig. 116A) but cup-and-cover swellings soon became dominant, carved with gadrooning, acanthus leaf, and the like, the fluted shafts above often topped with Ionic caps (Fig. 116B). Heavy moulding edged the canopy and further carving filled the under-face of its panels, except when such wooden panels were omitted, their place taken by a "tester" of fabric stretched within the wooden cornice framework. This might be of embroidered velvet, for instance, matched by a silk-fringed velvet vallance. Some were of painted fabrics.

Fig. 116

Judging by old inventories, the hanging curtains also matched in colour but not necessarily in fabric. Tester, curtains, and vallance constituted the typical bed furnishings to be listed in a seventeenth-century inventory, and special sets of black curtains for mourning occasions were frequently to be found: the Verney Memoirs give a reference (1640) to the great black bed "that travels about the family whenever a death occurs".

By the early seventeenth century the English bedroom still lacked such comforts as looking-glass, washing equipment, and wardrobe, but the majestic canopied bed was thoroughly established. These old oak panel-headed beds never reached the enormous height of the eighteenth century four-posters, although some were later increased in height to suit loftier rooms. Nevertheless, with a height of seven or eight feet a bed might weigh several hundredweight.

Henry VIII's bed referred to above had a head piece of walnut gilded and silvered. Walnut was used more widely for beds than for any other "oak period" furniture, but the great majority were of the commoner wood, so sturdy that many an early-seventeenth-century specimen remains to this day. By the later years of the seventeenth century, however, such excessively heavy "sealed" beds with wooden canopies were already going out of fashion. By the beginning of the eighteenth century the fabric hangings had once more become all-important.

Early in the seventeenth century a few magnificently upholstered beds of Italian workmanship entered this country, but it was not until after 1660 that the Continental fashion became established. Its effect was to place such emphasis upon the lavish curtains that the posts of the bed became entirely hidden and therefore no longer merited embellishment. Indeed, in 1673, the diarist Evelyn commented that the Italians themselves were discarding wood in favour of bedsteads of "forged iron gilded" which offered no crevices for parasites.

Throughout the late Stuart period the principal bedrooms were arranged *en suite* with the other formal apartments in the fashionable new houses, and therefore of necessity were equally lofty. Celia Fiennes, in her late-seventeenth-century diary, comments upon one result of this, seen in Newby Hall,

Ripon, where, in the lofty bedrooms, "most of ye beds were two foote too low wch. was pitty they being good beds".

In such a setting the bulbous pillars and low canopy of the Elizabethan bed were utterly dwarfed: new designs had to be as much as sixteen or eighteen feet high and their proportions calculated to make them appear still taller; the new slender pillars were so long that on the average lathe they had to be turned in two parts and then inconspicuously joined. A yet greater impression of height was achieved by the use of tall finials at the corners of the cornice that held the fabric tester. Early examples, showing their Italian inspiration, might have fabric-covered knobs, reminiscent of the early Italian X-chair. By the end of the century great bunches of curling plumes were popular: they were mentioned in an inventory as early as 1666. Indeed, the 1626 inventory of Hatfield Priory refers to "i boxe with 8 fethers for ye bedds"—suggestive of plume decoration rather than an abbreviation of the "ffetherbedd and bolster" twice recorded in the list for the same chamber. Another Continental development was the use of carved and gilded cresting in fantastic elaborations above the cornice; below was draped the heavily-fringed vallance, and from the four corners and across the bedhead hung long, full curtains. The tester itself was covered in one of the multitudinous fabrics of the day—velvet, damask, or needlework—and more fabrics were glued to the wood of the deep, heavily-moulded cornice itself.

This style, again reminiscent of the X-chair, was much favoured by the Huguenot designer Marot who was noted for his gorgeous upholstery work, heavy tassels, and festoons of drapery. Evelyn recorded that the embroidery of Queen Mary's new bed cost £3,000.

Not even the heads of these beds were now panelled in the earlier style. Within the four-poster tent of fabric the bed itself was but a grand edition of the undraped low beds of the period, greatly resembling the beds of today. The square lines of head and end panels gave way to arch and double-ogee shapes at the turn of the century, and modes of decoration followed the various vogues for marquetry, lacquer, panels of caning, and exquisite walnut veneers. Queen Anne and early Georgian beds often had carved cabriole legs, and there was a fashion for inverted cabriole stumps instead of a foot-board. Some bedsteads around the turn of the century compromised with canopies extending over only half the area of the bed.

As the new eighteenth-century wood mahogany gradually ousted walnut from the more important rooms of fashionable houses, beds in the grand manner changed yet again. The style that now evolved was a modification of the previous vogue. The cornice, freed from its fabric covering, was now reduced to simpler, lighter, classic outlines. The posts were reduced in height, and while those at the head continued to be hidden behind the curtains, the foot-posts re-emerged into view. Consequently, while the head-posts were of plainly tapering square section in whatever hard wood might be available, the foot-posts were turned in slender, shapely lines with low relief carving on the slight thickening—vestige of the Elizabethan melon—above short cabriole legs.

As the eighteenth century advanced these cabrioles were replaced by square posts on plinth bases; Chippendale sometimes used lion-paw designs. Chippendale's simpler bed styles showed graceful pillars (Fig. 117), pierced cresting above the cornice, and pierced carving on the head-board. Of his more resplendent designs it is probable that few went further than the pages of his *Director*. It would take a brave craftsman to tackle the state bed with gilded dome for which he claimed "Magnificence, Proportion, and Harmony . . . a Workman of Genius will easily comprehend the Design".

Fig. 117

Domed canopies were popular at this period, for couches as well as beds; they were modified for the humbler home where a ring or "corona" in the French manner, suspended above the low, shapely bed-head, supported long folds of curtain.

Inevitably "Chinese" beds were devised around the mid-century, with pagoda-roof canopies and lattice head-boards, but even by the 1760's the classic mode was becoming established. Fluted foot-posts, for instance, swelled to graceful vase forms above the mattress level and tapered below to small spade plinths, with low-relief carving on the square faces (Fig. 118).

Decoration on Adam's homelier mahogany bed designs consisted largely of this reticent low-relief carving. His more magnificent state beds, however, were extravagant affairs of gilt and satin-wood and classical ornament, as befitted the domed ceilings and circular and elliptical rooms of his great houses. Indeed, the state beds of this period must have proved immensely satisfying to their opulent owners, despite the scorn of such connoisseurs as Walpole for a bed at Osterley Park "with eight columns, too theatric and too like modern head-dress, for round the outside of the dome are festoons of artificial flowers. What would Vitruvius think of a dome decorated by a milliner!"

Hepplewhite's persuasive influence is seen in many a well-proportioned bed characterized by careful detail and particularly shapely turned and reeded or fluted posts, often swelling to urn shapes. As on his chair legs, carved twists of ribbon might spiral down each post; others were carved with foliage, honeysuckle, husks, or wheat-ears, and in late work he sometimes used painted ornament. His cornices often followed bowed or serpentine outlines, their decoration carved, pierced, or inlaid. Upholstered head-boards were sometimes used.

Fig. 118

The "field beds" featured by Chippendale, Hepplewhite and their contemporaries continued to be made into the nineteenth century: the name indicated no more than that posts and tester could be taken to pieces and packed small. Sheraton showed a hinged example in his *Dictionary*.

Sheraton's exuberant imagination produced bed designs massed with tasselled, looping draperies, their ponderous domes topped with crowns, plumes, and pineapples (Fig. 119). But he suggested various attractive details such

Fig. 119

as well-proportioned pillars. By the end of the century, however, in both general proportions and ornamental detail bed designs were tending to sacrifice grace for weight. Large posts, heavily carved with leaves, pine-apples, and so on, were typical of this late manufacture, often with drapery and fruit carved on the head-board. The four-poster—itself a nineteenth-century term—died hard, but even by 1800 the tester was often omitted and the Continental vogue for metal fittings was resulting in a wealth of brass-work in and around the various joints, then regarded as the acme of hygiene. Many Regency beds were couch-shaped, with scrolling ends, their mahogany or painted wood lavishly decorated with applied brass-work.

From these it is a relief to turn to the simplicity of the cradle design which also underwent several distinct changes of fashion. Indeed, like the bed, the cradle was an important piece of display furniture throughout the sixteenth, seventeenth and eighteenth centuries, when a birth brought many congratulatory visitors.

Some of the earliest European cradles appear to have been open boxes suspended above the damp floor on end-posts of the vertical trestle type which permitted gentle rocking. An interesting example of this design is to be seen in the recently revealed medieval wall paintings at Longthorpe Tower, near Peterborough. These paintings probably date from a little before 1340, and show a cradle apparently suspended from two end verticals linked by a wide stretcher at floor level. By the sixteenth century, the cradle frame was more simply mounted on cross-bearers shaped as rockers which the mother could work with her foot. The cradles of Queen Elizabeth and James I were both solid panelled boxes enriched with carving and the latter also with inlay and touches of gilt. Little James I had five "rockers" to wait upon him.

In the late sixteenth century the design was somewhat elaborated and the sides, panelled like a chest, were increased in height around the baby's head to offer some protection from draughts. Wooden pins inserted horizontally at the sides could be laced with cords to keep baby and bedding in position, while somewhat similar vertical-turned

seventeenth-century hanging
›oard decorated with carving,
.ding the guilloche motif on
.ide, and with traces of inlay.
open door panels, suggestive
he stone mason's work, are
with turned spindles.

b. A less ambitious oak hutch. An attempt has been made at mitred mouldings around the panels but those to the sides still show the chamfering of outdoor stonework. The position of the dowel pegs proves that the mouldings are part of the solid wood of rails and muntins.

A typical high quality eighteenth-century dresser design, in oak with drawer fronts of mahogany. The well-shaped frieze below the cornice is matched by the vertical shelf supports. Cupid's bow friezes link the drawers to the turned pillars above the low pot-shelf which is mounted on bracket feet.

finials at the corners gave a neat finish to what was usually a thoroughly well-made family heirloom. Good examples were carved and often dated and many were painted and gilded.

In the late years of the seventeenth century the design was developed so that a complete hood covered the head end of the cradle, sometimes with turned balusters at the sides. For ease of access to the baby the whole hood usually folded back on hinges. Some four-legged cribs were constructed entirely of turned spindles. Evelyn refers to many rural cradles plaited of lime and willow twigs, and even among the aristocracy wicker eventually came to have a considerable vogue.

Mahogany cots of the mid-eighteenth century tended to follow traditional lines but with more daintily curving hoods. Miniature four-posters had long been made for children, and during this century more cots on legs were also used. The major development, however, was the return of the hanging crib. This appears to have been re-discovered in early Georgian days, but it only became fashionable in Hepplewhite's time. The typical design consisted of two carved posts about four feet high connected by a rail and mounted on spreading "horse" legs. The cradle itself, of canework framed in wood, swung between the posts. In place of the hood a curtain might be draped from a carved and shaped upright. Sheraton, the ingenious, planned a swinging cradle that would continue in motion for ninety minutes by means of a clock-spring attachment.

10

STORE CUPBOARDS

IN medieval England, only the rich could afford the furniture made by a skilled carpenter. Cottagers had to depend on the rough, inferior work of the huchier or ark-wright, who was incapable of making anything more elaborate than an ark, or chest, or the equally primitive hutch. Indeed, there was little enough to distinguish the one article from the other during the thirteenth and fourteenth centuries. The hutch, forerunner of all later cupboarding, was just an extra-broad chest built of primitive riven oak planks, either up-ended or turned on its side so that the pivot-hinged lid came to the front as a door. Big, clout-headed nails fastened sides to top and bottom, and the door, a single slab of wood, was usually restricted to the central portion of the front. Shelves were sometimes fitted, held by pegs or nails driven horizontally into their ends from outside the hutch. Legs frequently raised fourteenth-century examples above the cottage floor; some authorities apply the term hutch only to this type.

Long wrought-iron strap hinges ending in simple rosettes were decorative alternatives to the more obvious pivot hinges, and strengthened the door against warping and splitting; stout strips of leather were also used. Fastenings consisted of wooden turn-buckles and locks.

By the fifteenth century carving had considerably replaced iron-work in furniture decoration. On hutches showing primitive construction methods the carving is frequently extremely crude and many examples are therefore credited with unduly early origin. When Henry VIII dissolved the monasteries (1520-40) and brought Italian craftsmen to England, he prepared the way for the new style of art and learning known as the English Renaissance. The carpenter was enormously influenced by the change, but the huchier, it has generally been assumed, continued to follow the older Gothic traditions of his forebears. Many very simply constructed hutches show poorly executed attempts at the late Perpendicular Gothic tracery of the fifteenth to early sixteenth centuries as their only ornament. This was pierced through their rough-hewn boards, thus further weakening a form of construction so poor that skilled craftsmen had begun to replace it with the framed-up panel design even by the fourteenth century.

An interesting alternative suggestion had been made by Cescinsky, that the cruder type of "post-Dissolution Gothic" piercing may be considerably later than the hutch itself—in any case hard to date with exactitude—added after the strong carpentering traditions of the fourteenth-sixteenth centuries had been lost. Undoubtedly much early furniture was adequately beautified with colour—greens, blues, reds, yellows, applied in paint or tempera.

The best oak hutches of the early Tudor period do show the newer panelled method of construction described in Chapter 1, whereby panels were fitted into a grooved framework of upright and horizontal stiles, rails and muntins. Mortise-and-tenon joints were secured by oak dowel pins driven into holes through all three thicknesses of wood, and shelves were similarly held without requiring glue. The top of the hutch might project in shaped moulding, and corner stiles were often continued to form plain or slightly-moulded square legs below the enclosed portion. Some hutches were completely divided horizontally into two or even three sections, each with its own small door, and occasionally separated by a row of drawers.

Fig. 120

In the late fifteenth and early sixteenth centuries linen-fold panelling was in vogue and varieties of this design were used on all sides of some good quality hutches. The more elaborate parchemin panel was an early sixteenth-century development, followed by early Renaissance motifs. Such carving largely took the place of paint, although Henry VIII possessed "a cupboard of waynscott coloured green and red".

Fine workmanship is sometimes found on an old credence cupboard—the small cupboarded table designed for church use to hold the eucharistic elements but often, apparently, employed by the laity in early times as a side-table for venom-tasting. The typical shape (Fig. 120) showed canted sides narrowing to the front, sometimes ornately carved.

In the early years of the sixteenth century, let it be emphasized, the hutch, a uniquely English piece of furniture, might be termed an aumbry but seldom yet a "cupboard". For until about 1550 the so-called cup-board was in fact a board or table set aside as a place on which to stand the drinking vessels during meals and, on important occasions, to display them in sufficient quantity to emphasize the wealth and status of their owner. For example, in 1530 Henry VIII had a "cup-board with ij small ambries in yt" indicating a side table fitted with cupboarding. Even then the new use of the word was creeping in, however: *vide* Palsgrave's reference the same year to a "cupborde to putte meat in".

The side table with shallow aumbries for storing plate under the table top or with a second shelf nearer the floor, buffet-fashion, was obviously but a convenient variation of the simplest cup-board of the day. But in noble households something more was required for displaying the plate, and in this case the cup-board might be replaced by a set of open shelves, receding like a flight of stairs and heavily draped with cloth. On the Continent and to a lesser degree in England, rules of etiquette decided according to rank precisely the number of tiers allowed.

The basic change in the use of the word cupboard dates from the mid-sixteenth century. As skilled craftsmen from the monasteries sought secular employment and learnt new ways from Italians and Flemings, furniture construction began to show marked improvements. In the case of cupboards, there were several important parallel developments. From the everyday hutch developed numerous storage cupboards of more specialized uses, which soon came to be known by that name; by early in the seventeenth century ordinary "close" or "joyned" cupboards were plentiful in large houses.

At the same time, from the old type of open cup-board and the early form of low dresser developed furniture basically intended for display—the farmhouse dresser in its later form and the ornate buffet which in turn gave place to the side-table of the late seventeenth century and the side-board of a century later. And from a combination of the buffet cup-board and the "cupboard with ambries" developed the most imposing display cupboard of all, the court cupboard—a typically Elizabethan and early Stuart product which, like the buffet, lost its identity after the Restoration. These display pieces—buffet, court cupboard, dresser, and sideboard—will be considered in the next chapter.

Only the rich houses had court cupboards and buffets; the dresser continued to betoken considerable means. But before the end of the sixteenth century every household with any pretensions at all had its various storage cupboards. Of these, the livery was one of the most necessary. In Tudor homes dinner and supper were generally eaten in common, but in addition liveries of food and lighting materials for the night were provided individually for each member of the household. While enclosed cupboards were scarce these were set out each day on the old open cup-board. Automatically, then, when this became enclosed with doors the name was transferred to the new piece. A large house would have not only a cupboard in which to set out the liveries but a small livery cupboard for each individual's sleeping quarters.

By Elizabethan days these cupboards had become attractive pieces, plainly constructed on the framed-up principle and often decorated with innumerable small ventilation holes, probably often backed with cloth, and elaborate carving. The first half of the seventeenth century began to show the more restrained geometrical ornament, but country work continued to feature occasional heavy floral and figure decoration and the typical Renaissance arch motif. Inlays of ivory and native woods helped to compensate for the lack of the earlier colour. These were applied in simple geometrical and floral patterns—at a period when the Continent was already enjoying the infinitely more ambitious styles of veneer and marquetry.

Good quality work of the seventeenth century showed fine outlines, important use of mouldings, and elaborate inlay, reflecting the classicism in the architecture of the time. A shaped plinth, or a moulding attached to suggest a plinth, often reflected the lines of the moulded cornice around the top and gave balance to the essentially square simplicity of the piece. Rather later Stuart decoration included the typical turned pieces split in half lengthways and glued to the stiles, applied mouldings and carving which was little more than repetitive incised scrollwork. While turning was popular, around the mid-seventeenth century, the cupboard front often consisted of one or two rows of vertical turned balusters instead of piercing for ventilation. At first these were bulbous but soon the more typical vase form was achieved. Ball turning was used during the Cromwellian period, when cupboards followed the contemporary fashion for projecting instead of sunken panels.

Elaborately smithed wrought-iron hinges of the period 1560-1640 may have been suggested by renowned German work. Scroll-shaped cock's-head designs were often used; a plainer wedge or butterfly style was a substitute. After about 1575 a plain H was sometimes introduced, occasionally engraved. Mid-seventeenth-century hinges were frequently of the small butt type attached inside the door, necessitated by the use of doors the full width of the cupboard front. These hinges were hand-made and not counter-sunk for screws.

The individual livery cupboard passed out of use after the Restoration, bedrooms often being fitted with corner cupboards which, as more or less architectural features, will be considered separately. "Dole cupboards", however, continued in both churches and large houses, holding the food set aside for the poor. These were often extremely handsome, with elaborate carved strapwork and the like. A late use of the old meaning of cup-board is seen in the open shelving of Jeremiah Bright's "dole cupboard" given to Ruislip church in 1697.

Some store cupboards of this period, like contemporary chests, were made with one or two drawers at the bottom, and additional dummy drawer fronts were sometimes inserted, in contrast to the early chests of drawers which took on the appearance of cupboards with doors enclosing their drawers. These "drawing tills" were very occasionally featured even in the early Tudor days.

After the Restoration, cupboards for all purposes continued to be made, particularly for kitchen use, but, as oak gave place to walnut as the favourite wood, cabinets, bureaux, bookcases, chests of drawers and tallboys answered more specifically many of the requirements previously met by the plainer piece.

Another resemblance to contemporary mule chests and early chests of drawers was seen in the farmhouse piece of about 1660 which consisted of a cupboard with a couple of half-width drawers beneath it raised on baluster-turned legs following the lines of the corner stiles. This piece had waved stretchers or sometimes a shelf a little above floor level.

Another type of ventilated food cupboard dating from as early as the sixteenth century is occasionally found with a sloping top: this is generally regarded as a game cupboard (Fig. 121). The farmhouse bacon cupboard also dates from early times, containing hooks on which to hang cured flitches. During Cromwellian days it developed a character of its own, the doors of the shallow cupboard forming the back of a fireside settle with arms and box seat. Often boasting a moulded cornice or additional storage space above the main cupboard, this handsome piece of furniture continued in oak, elm, fruit-woods, and brown-stained pine until about 1725 (Fig. 122). Then the simple cupboard form returned to favour, being produced in large quantities for another hundred years.

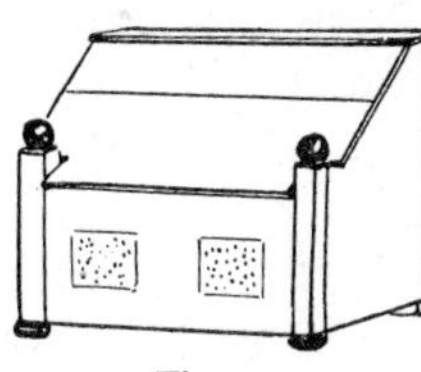

Fig. 121

Fig. 122

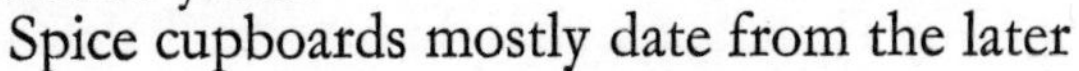

Spice cupboards mostly date from the later

years of the seventeenth century—delightful little square cupboards for hanging on the wall, liberally decorated and fitted with drawers to hold spices or small medicaments.

Apart from food and dining room requirements, clothing and linen were the principal items to be stored in pre-Restoration England. The forerunner of the wardrobe was the press, fitted either with pegs for hanging clothes or with shelves for linen. Smollett used the word wardrobe in its modern sense in 1753 but previously it was applied to the room where clothes were kept; clothes presses and clothes chests were apparently still the accepted terms for the cupboard-drawers construction.

As early as 1386 Chaucer mentioned "a press ycovered with a faldyng reed" (coarse red cloth), but they continued to be rare luxuries for another hundred and fifty years, and none appears to have survived that can be dated much earlier than Elizabethan times. But by the end of the sixteenth century they were becoming customary in large houses, and in 1600 J. Pory mentioned "each chamber hath a presse curiously painted and varnished"—possibly a hint of the later "japanning".

Painted furniture has always been particularly associated with the bedroom. In the late seventeenth century the press proved a tempting basis not only for "lacquer boards" imported from the East but for the imitation japanning that became a rage; the mid-eighteenth-century craze produced more cheaply japanned cupboards in the "Chinese" manner and others late in the century were painted with a multitude of flowers, ribbons, and trophies.

Early presses followed the lines of contemporary cupboards, being particularly deep, solid structures. After the Restoration they developed in very much the same way as the double chest of drawers, dating from about 1710, which came to be known as the tallboy. Until the end of the seventeenth century oak was still the accepted wood; and in conformity with contemporary room panelling the straight lines from top to bottom associated with earlier examples were lightened by a division rather below half-height. Above were two doors, often set within decorative side panels and topped by a handsome straight cornice. Balancing

By the later years of the eighteenth century mahogany wardrobes were in vogue. This example is notable for its intricate fret-cut cresting and cornice frieze. Applied mouldings are used to suggest panels on the front, the corner paterae matching the brass ring handles.

PLATE 29

An oak court cupboard wi
elaborate strapwork ar
deep-sunk panels; chequ
inlay to frieze and low she
and small chequer bandin
on cupboarding. Pillars wi
caps. About 1600.

Another example of early Stuart origin, with neatly executed strapwork, guilloche motif down the corner stiles, and the channel-moulded panel rails, part chamfered, part elaborately moulded.

this, the lower portion projected an inch or two at front and sides. Occasionally the corner stiles were continued to form legs; an alternative was a moulded plinth with brief ball, bun, or bracket feet.

The lower portion frequently appeared to consist of drawers so that the whole resembled a cupboard on a chest of drawers; but the hanging space was generally deeper than it looked and only the two long drawers at the bottom were genuine.

Walnut hanging cupboards of the late Stuart period with the swell below the cornice are scarce, built-in cupboards having provided ample hanging space. When mahogany came into more general use after 1750 presses were made of it in the earlier Queen Anne style. Many "bachelor" pieces consisted of sliding shelves fitted with baize to cover the contents within the upper portion which surmounted the drawers. Hanging cupboards on stands, like the chests of drawers on stands made in oak and walnut, were also made in mahogany, the baluster-turned leg giving place to the cabriole as the fashion changed. Not until the last thirty years of the eighteenth century were many wardrobes made with doors to the full height.

Features associated with the mid-eighteenth century included fret-cut cresting, Greek key and dentil cornice decoration, fine mahogany veneers bordered with curving applied mouldings to suggest a panelled front and carving on the canted front edges. A serpentine outline and enrichment of the bracket feet are associated with Chippendale's French style; later "Chippendale" examples might show the lower portion following the *bombé* silhouette of the contemporary commode, with similar use of ornate carving to the canted corners, feet, and frieze. Cornices might be straight or pedimented. Raised vertical flutes and the "peardrop" frieze were frequently used, and the moulds suggesting panels on the doors were straight instead of curving, their shaped corners often finished with carved rosettes.

Wardrobes designed in the Adam period between 1758 and 1792 might show low relief carving on the frieze with swags, vases, and other classical motifs. Inlay on the panels in contrasting woods was a late Adam feature much used in designs recorded by Hepplewhite and Sheraton. Indeed, Hepplewhite regarded the wardrobe as "an article of considerable consequence" and his *Guide* illustrated simple, well-proportioned examples in which elliptical or rectangular door panels of figured mahogany were surrounded by diagonally inlaid satinwood. Dentils were introduced on the cornice, flutes and pateræ on the frieze. Sheraton favoured the elliptical panel, introduced, for example, on the large break-front design popular after 1750. This wardrobe was divided vertically into three parts. The two sides, designed for hanging clothes, had doors opening the full depth from cornice to plinth, while the wide centre portion, stepped forward about six inches, was designed as a shelved clothes press with double doors above the chest of drawers below. From the outside, however, each of the three sections had the appearance of being a cupboard mounted on three rows of drawers. The wings were constructed each as a separate piece; the central portion in two parts. Cornice and frieze above and plinth below, each being in one piece and screwed to the various sections, combined the massive structure in one sturdy unit.

The less lavish wardrobe of the last quarter of the century, however, more frequently consisted merely of the central portion, constructed mainly of pine, with cornice, press shelves, and chest of drawers made separately; mahogany mouldings facing the cornice and around the top of the lower portion disguised the joints. The upper tray section, made of solid mahogany, had veneered doors showing fine mahogany figurings. Trays and drawer linings were of oak. In the eighteenth century a strip of convex moulding edged the locking door to cover the join with the second door; after 1800 it was more usually reeded. As on the tallboy, bracket feet, plain or in cabriole profile, or in the outward curve of the "French" style, were alternatives to a plain plinth base in the eighteenth century, followed in the nineteenth by ugly turned stump feet. Indeed, nineteenth-century wardrobes soon sacrificed beauty for massive proportions, but at least they could often boast of excellent workmanship and the finest grain veneers.

11

DINING ROOM DISPLAY FURNITURE

THE pride of the rich Elizabethan household was the buffet, the court cupboard or the approximation between the two which displayed and housed the family plate in the most splendid possible manner. It was suggested in the last chapter that the buffet was an obvious development from the side table—the cupboard in the pre-1550 sense of the word on which the family plate was arranged and from which drinks were served during meals (*vide* Harrison's *Description of Britain*, 1577-89). The word buffet has had several distinct uses but may be derived from the same association of ideas, from the past tense of the French verb *boire*, to drink (*il buvait*, he was drinking).

In lordly feudal households several extra tiers of shelves were required above the cupboard to array the plate on coloured, tasselled cloths or on the white damask which came into vogue late in the fifteenth century, etiquette ruling the number of tiers according to rank, from five for royalty down to one for unennobled persons of gentle descent. Such was the "riche cup-borde well and richly garnyshed" possessed by Henry VII's wife Elizabeth. At a banquet given by Henry VIII, two "cup-boards" reaching from roof to floor were covered in vases of gold. An inventory of the furniture of Sir Thomas Kyston, 1603, mentions "one little joined borde wt a fast frame to it, to sett on glasses. Itm, a thing like stayres to set plate on". Such a piece as the latter is illustrated in a volume published at Dilingen in 1587, describing ceremonies at Prague. This massive five-tiered example is cloth-draped but as plain in outline as an old mounting block with an extra broad bottom step.

Even by the fifteenth century the simplest type of buffet, with two additional open shelves under the table top, had been evolved, Lydgate's illuminated *Life of St. Edmund* depicting a crude example. But the standard design of conspicuously substantial buffet began its hundred years of popularity in the second half of the sixteenth century.

The appearance of great solidity in the three tiers of open shelving was achieved by deep-carved friezes, and the two tiers of richly-carved bulbous columns supporting them at the front and the wide flat posts at the back. In early examples, the bulbous "acorns" with their deeply-carved flowers and foliage often combined with voluted caps, produced a virile beauty from which something was lost in the development of the more elongated pear-shaped bulbs of the early seventeenth century. Very occasionally carvings of fabulous animals took the place of pillars in both buffets and court cupboards, but these suggest Continental work. The shelves themselves, held by dowel pins, showed deeply moulded edges, but were little more than half an inch thick; below, on front and sides, was a wealth of individualistic floral carving, inlay, or, occasionally, painted floral design. Around the central shelf bold gadrooning was often used; around the lowest shelf chequer patterns in different coloured woods. Frequently the front of one or both the upper shelves pulled out as a drawer on grooved runners. The back supporting posts showed simpler repetitive carvings such as chevrons or gadrooning. Sometimes feet were added, generally plain square or bun shapes but occasionally improved with volute carving.

As turning became popular in the seventeenth century the stumpy, bulbous column gradually assumed a more slender vase shape. By about 1620 it had lost its lavish carving and frequently resembled the baluster legs then appearing on other pieces of furniture, although in both buffets and court cupboards the earlier styles of flamboyant Elizabethan decoration lingered on in the early Stuart period, long after simpler pieces were reflecting the newer influences, French and Flemish, Dutch and Spanish, that swept across the Channel.

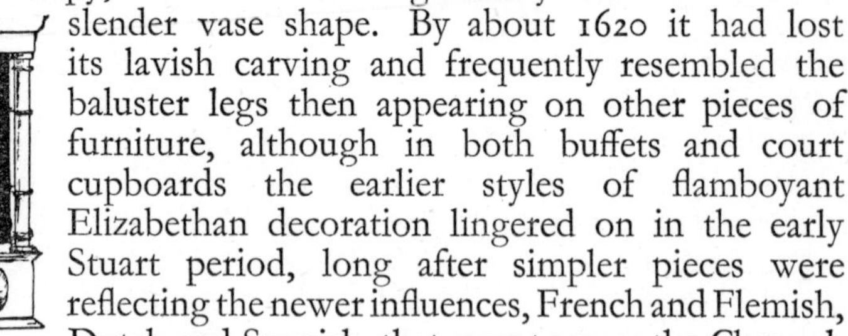

Fig. 123

Cluster-columns (Fig. 123) offered an alternative lighter treatment of the supports; they were in use during the middle years of the century while the customary glued-on decoration consisted of split turned balusters, egg shapes, and other simple motifs, often in willow wood dyed to resemble ebony. Other later seventeenth-century examples occasionally showed the single or even double twist-turn pillar, better suited to walnut than to oak and still popular in Queen Anne's reign.

Carving on seventeenth-century friezes had lost the Elizabethan exuberance and showed strips of formal repetitive design, often in great profusion but with little attempt at modelling; the finish of constructional details however—feet for instance—improved.

When storage as well as display was required, one tier of the buffet was sometimes partly enclosed. The most usual form was a canted cupboard between top and middle tiers, the centre portion of the cupboard, with a square door, being in line with the front of the buffet, the cupboard sides running back diagonally to the back corners of the buffet. An early alternative which returned to favour in the seventeenth century was a straight row of cupboards filling half the depth of the piece, still allowing plate to be displayed on the shelf in front of them. This deeply panelled square cupboard door, often on pivot hinges, and the panelling that sometimes backed the lower, open tier of such a buffet offered wonderful opportunities for lavish Renaissance carving on late Elizabethan and early Stuart examples, with deep-set arches, elaborate guilloche and acanthus surrounds, floral inlay, carved coats of arms.

A few buffets were made in walnut in both sixteenth and seventeenth centuries. Some showed bevelled panels and rich ivory and pearl inlay, but later seventeenth century examples were generally plain oak structures, depending on good workmanship, well-proportioned mouldings and simple applied geometrical motifs. Such were easily dispensed with when low cupboarded side-tables returned to favour soon after the Restoration, although a modified form is seen occasionally in an eighteenth century "waiter", a clumsy two-tier structure on castors.

The court cupboard contemporary with the later buffet was an extremely handsome piece, probably restricted to the richest houses in Elizabethan days but becoming more widespread later. It most closely resembled the type of buffet fitted with small canted cupboards in its upper portion, but was distinguished by straight-fronted, full-depth cupboards below. Probably the name (French, *court* for short) was at first only given to the upper portion as a separate unit.

Like the buffet, the Elizabethan court cupboard's chief enrichment was given to the magnificent bulbous supports of the heavily-carved cornice and the varied decoration on the doors and panels of the small upper cupboards. These followed the same fashions as seen on the buffet, with the same continuation of early forms, only a little modified, until the mid-seventeenth century. By then, however, many court cupboards had lost their distinctive pillars entirely, showing only vestigial pendant-turned knobs on the front corners of the cornice (Fig. 124).

Fig. 124

Early examples occasionally introduced carved heads or the atlantes and caryatides beloved of Renaissance carvers on the cornice corners and around the upper cupboard doors. The lower doors lent themselves to arch motifs and the stiles and rails to the many monotonous S-scroll patterns popular on Stuart work (Fig. 125).

Fig. 125

On the court cupboard as on the buffet, by this time, the small upper cupboard with canted sides was giving place to straight cupboarding with two doors often decorated with typical Cromwellian projecting panels. The doors of the lower cupboards frequently extended to the full width of the front, and instead of decorative butterfly, cock's head or H hinges, small butt hinges had to be used, attached inside the doors.

Some seventeenth-century examples were raised considerably above the floor on legs, turned at the front and square at the back. In this case the lower cupboards were reduced to half their usual height and finished with a shaped apron.

Like other high class furniture around 1600, court cupboards were made in walnut as well as the prevailing oak. Hatfield Priory inventory, 1626, listed "2 Court cupboards, j walnuttree, j wainscoate" in the lower gallery. The Earl of Northampton possessed three examples in 1614 among other walnut furniture.

Country carpenters continued to make court cupboards until the early years of the eighteenth century. Examples of the William and Mary period followed in the wake of the fashion for mitred mouldings, applied around elaborately shaped panels. At the same time an interesting development of the court cupboard was to be seen in Wales. Introduced in the sixteenth century, it soon became so popular that it took the Welsh name *cwpwrdd deuddarn*—two-piece cupboard. During the seventeenth, eighteenth and early nineteenth centuries, it continued to be made in oak, its decoration largely restricted to a well-designed arrangement of numerous panels, the restrained use of inlay which continued when England was favouring veneers and marquetry, and carving of inter-lacing Celtic motifs on uprights and lower rail.

The most notable development, however, dates from early in the seventeenth century when the three-piece *cwpwrdd tridarn* was developed, with the addition of an extra tier of open shelving for the display of pewter and earthenware or to store the week's baking. Pillars—rare specimens showing the bulbous form—sometimes supported this topmost canopy, at a period when only turned pendant knobs recorded the earlier use of corner supports in the middle section. In less elaborate examples solid side uprights with a waved outline balanced the shaped frieze on the top cornice.

Another far less lavish piece of furniture having much in common with the buffet and court cupboard was developed contemporaneously in Wales as in other country districts—the dresser. The Welsh dresser had a pronounced cornice finished with corner pendants, projecting above the shelving—an obvious link with the court cupboard—and either cupboarding or a pot rack, *pobbwrdd*, below.

The name dresser has been given to many different pieces

of furniture, and the word had literary mention as early as 1420. A 1562 reference describes the beating of a drum to warn "gentlemen of the household to repaire to the dresser". It is probably simplest, however, to restrict it to those pieces on which, in the country living-room-kitchen, the family plate was "dressed" or arrayed. It then takes its proper place as a variant of the early cupboarded side-table which developed a character of its own when open shelving, development of "a thing like stayres" referred to above, was stood upon it or fastened to the wall above for the greater display no longer of cups but of plates.

It appears that the plain flat table top of this fundamentally less-ornate piece long continued adequate, however, to display the pewter table ware that came into more general use in place of the older treen (wooden) necessities towards the end of the sixteenth century. Indeed, it is often obvious that the typical mid-seventeenth-century dresser, resembling a cupboarded side-table, has been aggrandised in a farm-house kitchen by the addition of open shelves or plate racks such as were made separately in the eighteenth century. Backboards were invariably later additions. When a dresser was used in a large establishment it was only in the servants' quarters. Hatfield Priory had a "side bourd" in the hall but a "dresser board" in the kitchen.

Late seventeenth-century examples were raised on a number of twist or baluster-turned legs with either an open shelf or turned or waved stretchers below a waved—often cupid's bow—frieze, much like contemporary chests of drawers and store cupboards on stands. The resemblance was increased by the frequent introduction of small spice drawers in the frieze. The two back legs were plain and cost was sometimes reduced by the use of flat legs at the front cut out in baluster profile. Handles were small wooden knobs, sometimes facetted, brass pear-drops or drop-loops.

By the beginning of the eighteenth century dressers were commonly made with open shelving and sometimes small cupboards as well above the table portion. Below the table top, north country dressers were most usually fitted with cupboards, or both cupboards and drawers, on bracket feet. The finest had shaped door panels, the early ones being semi-

typical example of good country workmanship in oak of the early eighteenth ntury, the court cupboard pillars reduced to pendant knobs. The panels are oulded and splayed in an architectural manner, and above and below the lower cupboards are glued-on mouldings.

a. This typical late-eighteenth-century example shows the mahogany sideboard then most popular. The front is in serpentine outline and the decoration includes lines of stringing, pendant diminishing husks, and fan spandrels under the central drawer.

b. By the end of the century heavier sideboards with solid pedestals were agai in vogue. In this bow-fronted example, finely veneered in mahogany, th pedestals are fitted with wine coolers. About 1800.

circular, later more often ogee-shaped. An alternative was a row of deep drawers and a shelf near the floor for pots. Oak was the usual wood, occasionally decorated with cross-banded walnut borders.

The simplest cottage dresser, often made in fruit-woods, consisted of no more than a row of drawers under the table top, set upon four plain square legs, and with the plain open shelving above topped by a simple moulded frieze. At the opposite extreme was the expensive Queen Anne dresser veneered in beautiful burr walnut with small cupboards, sometimes with arched doors, to the sides of the lower shelves above the table. The cornice then showed contemporary mouldings, and the cornice frieze was shaped to match the framing under the drawers. For a time there was a fashion for elaborate pierced patterns, followed by a preference for a plain straight cornice towards the end of the eighteenth century. The front legs were in cabriole shape—on oak dressers as well as walnut, and on some of the comparatively few in mahogany.

While the farmhouse dresser continued the traditions of the buffet, post-Restoration gentility favoured a return to the earlier simple side-table in the dining room. Before the Restoration this most direct descendant of the old cup-board was typically a small oak table on turned legs lightly constructed with one or two drawers, without locks, and with their sides grooved for runners, plainly inserted in the frieze. The name side-board, like cup-board, was introduced when board was still a usual term for table. With only small constructional changes, this design continued through the seventeenth century and into the eighteenth, at first in oak and then also in walnut.

The Tatler in 1710 suggested that " the sumptuous Side-board to an ingenuous Eye has often more the Air of an Altar than a Table", and by the time mahogany was becoming popular for tables in the 1730's it had come to be regarded as an important architectural feature. But it was still primarily a table. Such designers as William Kent favoured very solid, massive construction, with heavy scroll legs, often grouped in threes, or elaborately carved cabrioles richly gilded. Some towards the mid-eighteenth century showed the serpentine form, the fret carving around the frieze, above an acanthus leaf design on the shapely apron, the cabochon knee, and the finely detailed beadings of early "Chippendale" work. After about 1735 such "side-board tables" were often topped with a material called scagliola—a cement-like mixture of calcined gypsum, isinglass, and Flanders glue coloured to resemble marble, which, when set, could take a very high polish. But, without so much as a single drawer, they were still a far cry from the late eighteenth century sideboard and they were sufficiently distinctive to be continued when the latter was developed, usually with plain mahogany tops.

The first move towards the sideboard was the addition of small detached pedestal cupboards, one on either side of a long, six-legged table (Fig. 126). On these stood urns, occasionally of japanned copper, more often of mahogany lined with lead and fitted with taps. To support large plates, a simple brass rail about twelve inches high was fitted at the back of the table. Sheraton may occasionally have favoured, but did not originate, the use of little green silk curtains on the rail. His designs for brasswork were often elaborate, including fitments for candles to give full beauty to the plate below.

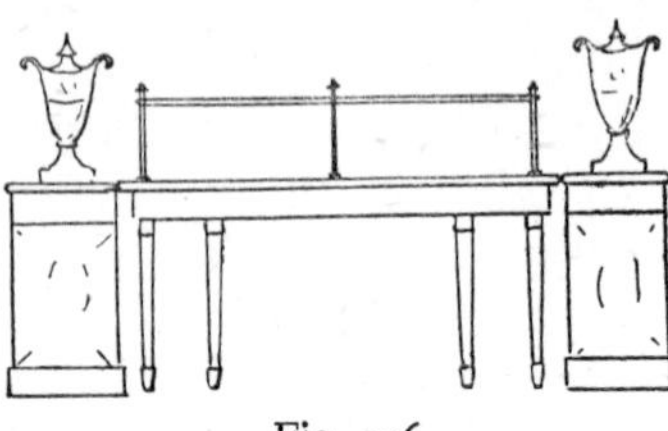

Fig. 126

Robert Adam is generally given credit for this side-table design which bore the stamp of his classical style. It is probable that both Chippendale and Hepplewhite made them to his plans. Not until nearly 1770 did pedestals and table become one unit, frequently fitted with drawers in the frieze and often also in place of cupboards in the pedestals (Fig. 127). Quadrant-shaped, three-legged tables sometimes served a similar purpose and date from about 1770.

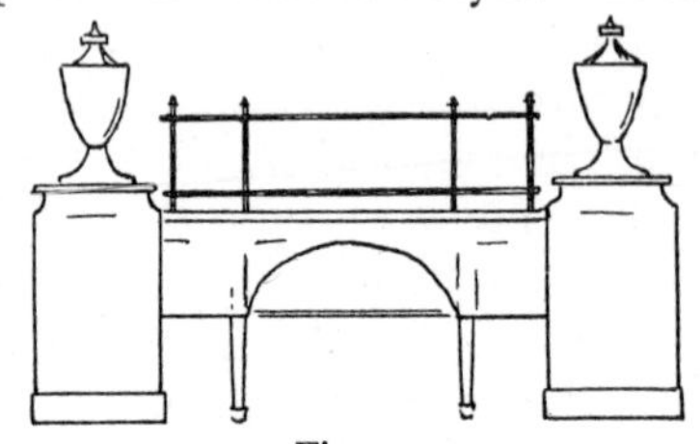

Fig. 127

The various parts of this sideboard helped to overcome the difficulties arising in old houses from the distance between dining room and kitchen. One pedestal might be lined with tin and fitted to keep plates hot, the drawers of the other lined with lead to hold bottles of wine, or even water for rinsing glasses. One urn became a knife and fork box, the lid raised by a central tube until the shape was changed to the more convenient octagonal; the other perhaps a container for ice. Such a unit might be augmented by a brass-hooped mahogany wine cooler, placed under the centre of the sideboard. Typical Adam design was of sarcophagus shape, with ring handles suspended from lion-head plates, and lion-paw feet. Urns were often omitted from the design, sometimes being replaced by square knife boxes with sloping tops, and after about 1770 the heavy solidity of the pedestals gave place to smaller cupboards or drawers each raised on four turned or tapering legs, although pedestal cupboards continued to be made. The sideboard legs became shorter as more fitments were added—often including a secret drawer—but space in the centre was reserved for the wine cooler or cellaret. The corners under the central table and drawers were usually decorated with inlaid arched brackets or fan-shaped spandrils and occasionally, in Sheraton designs, there was a central tambour cupboard with sliding shutter (Fig. 128). Drawer pulls were of brass, with moulded and chased roses, until the late 1770's when stamped brass backplates began to be made.

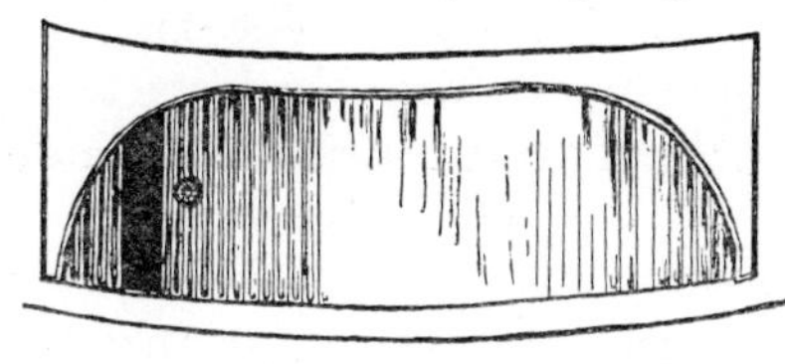

Fig. 128

The small sideboard consisting of no more than a single shallow drawer flanked by a square cupboard or drawer on either side and raised on the tapering fluted legs of the period, seldom dates from earlier than about 1780 (Fig. 129). Occasionally an earlier example is found, however, on square, robust legs and vigorously carved with "Gothic" motifs.

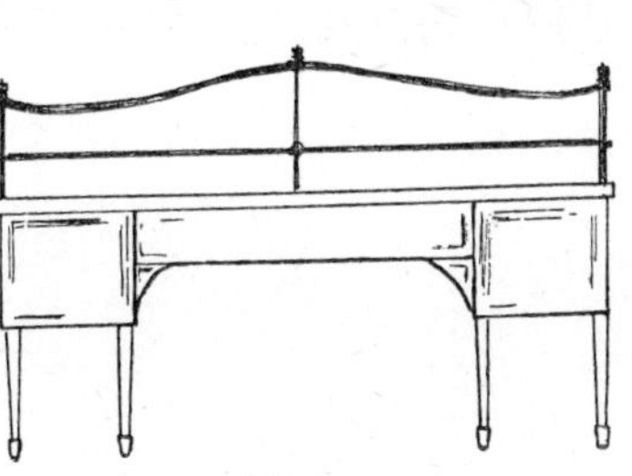

Fig. 129

Serpentine, bow, and even concave shapes may date from 1770 onwards, the bow slightly after the serpentine and both credited to Hepplewhite. Robert Adam often planned a semi-circular recess in a dining room to hold a sideboard shaped to fit. Such designs necessitated superlative workmanship and this was reflected in the rich inlays of satin-wood and borders of tulip-wood and in the decorative flowers, urns, fans, ribbons, and other more or less classical motifs inlaid and painted at this period. Sheraton in his *Drawing Book* suggested that the concave shape was unusual, but might "secure the butler from the jostles of the other servants".

The Hepplewhite style often showed a serpentine front with concave corners, and square, tapering legs, sometimes inlaid; Sheraton preferred convex lines and his later work more often suggested turned reeded legs. The average Georgian sideboard, six or seven feet long, had six legs, four in front and two at the back, but there was considerable variety.

By the end of the century sideboards had been fitted with slides for serving trays and every variety of cupboarding, shelves and racks, while yet retaining a grace of form which was lost early in the nineteenth century in a gradual return to a heavier version of the solid pedestal shape (Fig. 130). Delicate inlay gave place to ponderous carving and the late Sheraton designs with their insistent lion masks, "massive ornamented legs, and moulded frames" were only outdone by some of the unwieldy "Empire" creations that followed.

Fig. 130

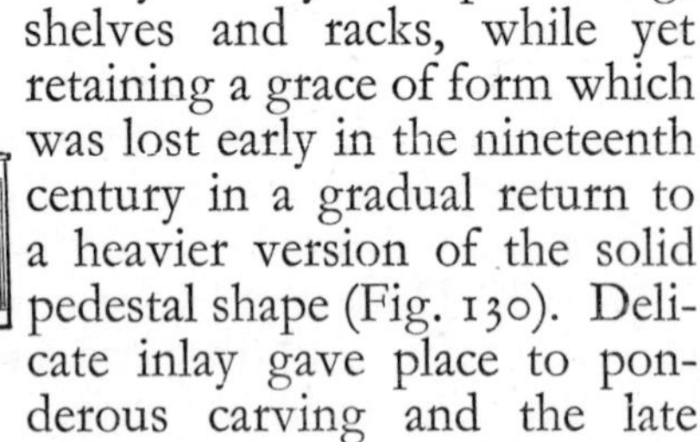

A William III desk of walnut
eered on oak, with herringbone
ıldings. The line of moulding
ɔss the front and the deep well
bove are relics of earlier design.

b. In this early type of desk the flap opens on to two gate-legs. There is a well sunk in the top. The legs show the baluster turning of typical gate-leg tables and the stretcher construction of the late seventeenth century.

c. By the mid-eighteenth century the vogue had been established for such solid mahogany desks. The serpentine front called for fine workmanship, requiring little decoration beyond the rococo mounts.

The early post-Restoration form of tall, fall-front walnut bureau or escritoire mounted on a stand. The drawers have mitred corners to their veneer borders and a particularly fine burr walnut veneer appears on the central cupboard.

12

CABINETS AND BUREAUX

LONG before man began to think of comfort in his home he felt the need of a safe place for his valuables. When chest or coffer constituted most of his movable furniture, he partitioned off a corner as a small "till" or "purse". In Tudor and Stuart days the oak or elm "Bible box" was popular, especially after the publication of the Authorized Version in James I's reign. But even this box was really nothing more than a diminutive plank chest with a stout lock and sometimes, late in the period, a drawer at the bottom.

In the farm or merchant's home this might house a variety of documents and valuables, but, even before the seventeenth century, was proving inadequate to meet the needs of a more civilized society. Writing requirements, in particular, necessitated a modification of the design: the lid was given a slight slope and hinged at the top to resemble the small desks (*armariola*) which old manuscripts show to have been in use since early times in church and monastery. Tiny drawers were fitted inside, illuminists using them to hold their bags of colours.

After 1650 such boxes were occasionally referred to as bureaux, a word originally associated with rough woollen cloth, forerunner of the baize used on some tables to this day. Both chairs and tables covered with "bayes" appear in seventeenth-century inventories.

At the same time, while the small Bible box was assuming the more elaborate style of the bureau, the larger chest was becoming transformed to meet a similar need, among the well-to-do, for tiny drawers, cupboards, and pigeon holes assembled in much greater profusion behind locked doors. The result was the English-made cabinet, small at first but soon comparable with those lavishly ornate creations that had long been the pride of Cotinnental nobility. After centuries of rivalry between "carpenter" and "joiner", there is contemporary reference to the trade of "cabinet-maker" as early as 1660. In an eighteenth-century England discovering the fascination of collecting precious trifles, cabinet and bureau dominated furniture design.

Rare examples of dated cabinets as early as 1650 show obvious Continental inspiration. Seventeenth-century designs for these luxurious furnishings clung to the plainly rectangular lines of the earlier chest, often topped by heavy, straight cornices and mounted on tall stands. Some mid-century examples showed the pronounced cornice, jutting panels, string-of-bead or similarly turned legs and stretchers associated with Cromwellian oak. Other massive specimens were inlaid with mother-of-pearl, bone or ivory, in the Spanish manner. Purposeless mouldings and a variety of split turnings and bosses were sometimes glued to plain oak cabinets before oak and its traditional treatments began to give place to walnut and the lighter Continental fashions brought by Charles II and his court.

Cabinets of 1670 onwards still held to the chest shape but were less massive.A drawer was often featured in the cornice frieze, often a swelling, pulvenated frieze. Another row of drawers appeared in the frieze of the stand, frequently made of elm wood, above shapely turned legs—some twist-turned —flat stretchers, and ball or bun feet. As in the case of the contemporary chest of drawers on stand, the stand followed the style of other side tables and was gradually reduced in height. Two vertical doors usually embraced the entire front of the cabinet and displayed particularly fine lock-plates. The space within was wholly occupied either by drawers or by a combination of drawers, cupboards, and pigeon holes.

By the reign of William III even the uses of cabinets were becoming more specific and designs more diverse. One variety, now rare, was the display cabinet, with glazed front. Samuel Pepys ordered what were perhaps the earliest glazed bookcases, as opposed to open shelving, recorded in his diary, July, 1666, and Queen Mary had several cabinets made for her collections of delft and Oriental porcelain. The plain rectangles of bevelled glass were fixed with brads and putty behind the heavy glazing bars of the period. These bars were usually of cross-grain walnut veneer, either in plainly rounded section, projecting above the level of the door surface and glued to narrower strips of oak (Fig. 131A), or in a flatter but more elaborate shape, in solid wood, with a square-cut fillet on either side (Fig. 131B). Not until near the end of the walnut period did the ovolo-moulded glazing bar become customary with a third fillet at the apex of the curve (Fig. 131C).

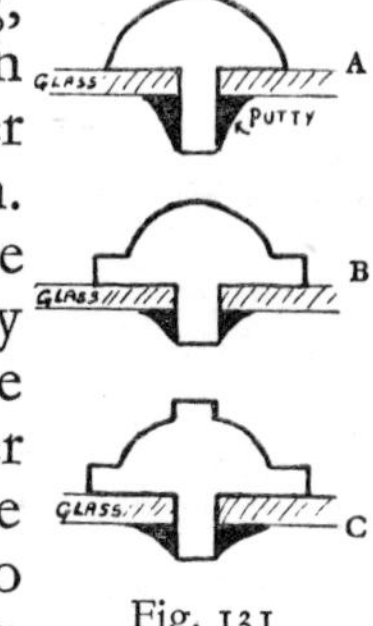

Fig. 131

While some of these china or book cabinets were placed on rebated stands, another type had a lower section of shelved cupboards with either glazed or panelled doors, mounted on a plinth in the heavy architectural style of the period.

At the same time it is necessary to trace the parallel development of the writing bureau, closely associated with the various types of cabinets throughout the eighteenth century, and given an immense fillip by the establishment of a national postal service. At this period the walnut bureau with slanting top was being placed upon a gate-leg stand so designed that, when open, the front of the box, hinged now at the bottom, could rest upon the two gate-legs.

By 1680 the table was being replaced by the chest of drawers, with straight or shaped front, projecting plinth mould—to balance the projecting edges of the pre-1690 bureau—and bun feet or, rather later (and often a repaired feature), projecting brackets. The well-constructed drawers were oak lined; after about 1690 they were wholly of oak and fitted with dust boards between the drawers. The mouldings on and around them changed with the corresponding fashions on other chests of drawers. Some of these chests of drawers were of the knee-hole design; occasionally they had pull-out writing slides resting on narrow oak bearers. Some, indeed, now rare, and dating from early Restoration years, were made on Continental lines with half the top folding back and the top "drawer" front falling open to constitute complete writing desk units in themselves.

The writing box, still a separate piece, also became more elaborate, the slant of the flap steeper and the interior fittings, like those of other cabinets, charmingly designed. The concave curving fronts of the small drawers were shaped from solid wood, those at the sides projecting slightly farther forward than those towards the centre, where domed pigeon holes flanked a little domed cupboard that often held a secret compartment behind tiny decorative pilasters.

Not for perhaps another five years did the chest and box become a single unit, applied moulding around specimens at the turn of the century remaining as a legacy of the earlier fashion and often masking a secret well for papers, a design discarded by the end of Queen Anne's reign. Chains or brass elbow-jointed stays supported the open deskflap; alternatively, small oak bearers, square at first, then matching the depth of the top drawers which replaced the early well, could be pulled out by tiny brass handles. These were slotted into the chest framework immediately below the flap hinges. The inside of the desk flap, decorated to match the outside, was occasionally fitted with a square of velvet.

At the same time, other writing boxes, at first in oak, then in walnut, were more simply mounted on legs without drawers and resembled some of the first toilet mirror boxes which arrived from the Continent at the turn of the century. Early legs were turned and tapering, such as the peg-top shape, linked by flat, waved stretchers, with arching apron and bulbous feet; after about 1705 cabriole legs continued the graceful curves of the fret-cut apron.

The third major development of the late seventeenth century from the basic cabinet design was the combination of cabinet and bureau, known on the Continent from the sixteenth century. At first, the cabinet retained its rectangular chest shape, with the deep cornice, wide frieze and array of interior drawers and pigeon holes already described.

Later, in the eighteenth century, came the heavy architectural pediment harmonizing with the pilasters flanking the central cupboard, and below, the bureau-chest of drawers construction. Workmanship throughout is extremely fine. About 1745-50.

Lacquered bureaux of the Queen Anne period expressed the current vogue for arching lines. This example shows the typical deep cavetto mould to the curves of the broken pediment, rounded tops to the mirrored doors, and serpentine apron above heavy ball feet.

Instead of cupboard doors, however, this design opened with a wide fall-front hinged at the bottom, and presenting, when open, a writing flap similar to that on the bureau. Although sometimes mounted on a stand, such a bureau-cabinet was more frequently found on a chest of drawers.

Contemporaneously, from the 1680's, came the most elaborate variant of all: the china or book cabinet mounted upon a bureau; in this case the latter had slanting bureau flap and drawers below.

When this piece was intended for books rather than a display of porcelain, pigeon holes for ledgers and papers were included in the shelving, for books were comparatively rare until later in the century. The doors, usually two on the typical forty-two-inch width and one on the narrow twenty-four-inch width, were therefore not glazed; instead they were fitted with sheets of the Vauxhall mirror plate which began to be produced in quantity late in the seventeenth century and was distinguished by wide, flat bevels. During the late Stuart period the mirrors, the doors themselves, and the very heavy cornice above usually followed shapely curves such as double arch or double ogee.

Thus, by the early years of the eighteenth century, English furniture had become enriched by a range of handsome pieces from the simplest bureau on slender legs; through the heavier desk bureau; the simple cabinet on stand or on chest of drawers, and the combinations of bureau-cabinet; the glass-fronted display cabinet with shelves for books or china instead of tiny drawers; and the display cabinet united with bureau and chest of drawers.

With the exception of the simplest bureau, all these pieces lent themselves to the architectural furniture treatment of the period. Their close association with a chest on stand and tallboy is obvious: they were of necessity governed by the same principles of balance and proportion in relation to the tall, dadoed rooms they were designed to enhance. Many were made sufficiently narrow to stand against the piers of wall between the windows, but all offered expansive surfaces for the various types of decoration then in vogue.

Some cabinets were still plainly made in oak, without veneer, but many more were finely veneered in walnut, the backs in quality work being of panelled oak. A whole cabinet might be covered, inside and out, with small pieces of oyster veneer, often of olive or laburnum wood, or in burr walnut or some other decorative wood. Burr elm might be enhanced with bandings of foreign wood and further lightened with lines of stringing in wood or in the pewter specially associated with mulberry wood. A cabinet veneered in a fascinating assortment of native woods was sometimes given to the heir of a country estate upon his majority, as a record of the trees on the family lands.

In the reign of William, marquetry was lavishly applied, the wide flap of the bureau or bureau-cabinet lending itself particularly to this treatment. Early examples showed panels of realistic flowers, stiffly grouped; later work, flowing arabesques which sometimes entirely covered the piece. But soon after 1700 plain veneers returned to greater favour.

Lacquer work for all these pieces was immensely popular, both the high quality Oriental work and the less laborious paint-and-varnish imitations, executed entirely in England. The true Oriental product was known as "right Indian" or "right Japan"—the names used indiscriminately. Even this Oriental lacquer was largely made specifically for the European market. One rare English variety was incised, known as bantam work (from the Dutch settlement in Java). But the more usual method in good quality early English japanning was based on the gesso process of building up a ground of whiting and size which was then coloured, lac varnished, and gilded. In some cases the soft wood carcase of a cabinet was veneered in a light-grained wood—inside and out on the strong oak doors—to provide a lastingly smooth surface for the lacquer substitute. Black was most usual for the ground work; red comparatively rare; blue and white still rarer, for the more popular, enduring varnishes inevitably had a yellow tinge. Red and black were sometimes combined to produce a "counterfeit tortoiseshell" effect.

Until the vogue died in the 1730's many cabinets were produced in a distinctive plainly rectangular silhouette, lacking any cornice, and notable for elaborate lockplates and many fine hinges. Many of these were Oriental or Dutch, only their stands and matching cresting being English. These stands were richly carved, first in Italian Renaissance style with *putti*, crowns and so on, then the more restrained French style with tapering trumpet legs, the soft wood covered in gold or silver leaf. The low-relief gilded gesso around 1700 was followed by early Georgian stands resembling contemporary heavy side tables. On cabinets of this type elaborate pagoda roofs and plainer lacquered stands dated from the mid-eighteenth century. Pepys and Evelyn both recorded notable examples of early cabinets.

Whatever the decorative medium, however, all these pieces offered endless opportunities for the "cabinet maker" to show his skill in fine dovetailing, smoothly running drawers, slides and candle-rests and cunning secret compartments.

During the Queen Anne period the cornice was usually straight, built up layer by layer to achieve its elaborate profile and generally veneered in cross-grain walnut. The many varieties of broken pediment—angular, circular, swan-neck—began to be used in about 1715 and continued with only brief interruption throughout the century. They were important features on cabinets of all kinds that date from early Georgian days when mahogany was succeeding walnut in the principal rooms of fashionable homes. But it must be remembered that even the earlier oak and elm continued for simple bureau furniture well into the eighteenth century.

The extremely heavy architectural style favoured by William Kent coupled such pediments with classic pilasters on the stiles and cupboard doors and strap-work carving on cornice and pediment, sometimes painted and gilded, as in the built-in corner cupboard of the period.

The 1740's saw the introduction of lighter styles, however, Chippendale and his contemporaries exploiting the vogue for rich naturalistic carving on the frieze, on the apron of the stand, and down the square-cut legs. Bureau-cabinets continued the use of pilasters flanking the doors. But for about a decade the broken pediment was less popular than smaller straight designs, usually introducing dentil moulding. On the finest cabinets craftsmen of the Chippendale school placed fret-cut and pierced cresting boards; they gave considerable care to this detail, glueing several thicknesses of wood in different ways of the grain to avoid warping.

On bureau-cabinets the heavy mirror plates were replaced by fine panelling or clear glazing. Between 1740 and 1750 the fashion was for the glass to be framed in stiles with waved inner edges, perhaps carved with egg-and-dart borders. A similar effect was achieved on unglazed doors with narrow applied mouldings. Glazing bars until 1750 were always of the heavy ovolo mould but developments in the use of crown glass coincided with the fashion for the light graceful glazing bars which could safely be cut from the hard Spanish mahogany. These new bars, mostly in astragal section, built up in two parts and scarcely three-eighths of an inch wide, were introduced in innumerable patterns as the century progressed.

Cabinet furniture around the mid-century offered the master cabinet-makers wide scope for fantastic design in Chinese and Gothic styles. None of these designers made much attempt to be consistent in these themes, however. China cabinets, in particular, were obvious vehicles for bell-decked pagoda roofs and many fretted outlines. They were generally executed in soft wood, japanned and painted or partly gilded. More appreciated to-day are the mid-century desk-and-bookcase designs and the less ornate bureaux, desks, and writing tables, executed to the order of individual wealthy clients. These tended to be solid and workmanlike, much resembling the heavy pedestals of the early sideboards. Many bureaux were very similar to contemporary chests of drawers, either square or serpentine, with splay corners holding fluted pilasters or decorated with applied fret carving above bracket feet in cabriole outline. Under the flap a well-made bureau might show similar fret decoration on and around the little central cupboard and finely-fitted curving pigeon holes. Less happy were more elaborate "French" pieces with rococo ormolu mounts and fanciful feet instead of a plinth; Chippendale's published designs for feet were often complex and obscure.

By the mid-century bureaux and bureau-cabinets were

beginning to be made with special drawer fitments instead of oblique flaps. The top drawer in the chest of drawers section was then made to pull out slightly and, at the same time, fall open at the front as a horizontal flap, hinged at the bottom. This many-compartmented drawer was sometimes fitted with a board which could be tilted for writing.

It must be appreciated that the size and capacity, and therefore the complexity of the fitments, varied greatly throughout the eighteenth century. In the second half of the century some massive examples of both display and bureau cabinets, like later eighteenth-century wardrobes, were made in break-front designs. Others followed the lines of contemporary sideboards with elaborate curved fronts.

At the other extreme were dainty pieces such as a Chippendale "writing table and bookcase" which was but a cabinet on a table with a drawer fitted for writing and mounted on six tapering legs. Robert Adam is associated with the fashion for this elegant type of piece; at first the square of leather on the top was often surrounded on three sides with tiny drawers. Display cabinets might be as plain as contemporary corner cupboards, depending solely on the neat treatment of their glazing bars and general good workmanship for their effect of gracious drawing room charm.

Around the mid-century numerous designers were producing indistinguishable work, much of it based on earlier French designs such as those of Riesener, whom Shearer, for example, is thought to have followed. William Vile was particularly noteworthy for his superb craftsmanship. Hepplewhite's firm recorded a current appreciation of the serpentine curving apron linking bracket or out-curving feet. The classic style he followed was well suited to cabinet work.

Carving became slighter, more restful and generally limited to classic motifs. Often it overlapped the glass in a large piece, lightening its massive proportions. It was frequently replaced, however, by smooth panels of inlay and marquetry in classic designs dating particularly to the period 1770-80. After that, painting tended to usurp the more elaborate method. Straight cornices were crested with urn finials, swags, and so on. Pediments tended to be on a smaller scale, and pateræ were introduced on the friezes. After about 1770 the pear-drop cornice moulding was used repeatedly.

Just as the hanging corner cupboard of the later eighteenth century took the place of the large china cabinet in many a more homely room, so the smaller bureau or writing desk continued to fill the need met more grandly by the bureau-cabinet. This immensely varied piece followed the same changes as other cabinet furniture. Mahogany was most generally used, a particularly fine curl-patterned piece of Cuban wood being chosen for the flap, which had a lip-moulded edge. The inside compartments continued to be well made and included more or less secret hiding places, but they lacked the curving contours of earlier work. The small drawers were often fitted with ivory or bone handles. An occasional bureau was still made in oak for a cheaper market, sometimes banded with mahogany and with a conch shell motif inlaid on the flap.

Mahogany particularly suited all the various phases of eighteenth-century cabinets, the backs being panelled in mahogany or pine. But in the last quarter of the century the desire for colour in inlay and paint prompted the use of a certain amount of lighter satin-wood, both solid and veneered, on which contrast was typically achieved with bandings of richer-toned tulip-wood and light and dark lines composed of box-wood and ebony. Door panels and bureau flaps lent themselves to more elaborate designs. Late in the century ormolu mounts and Wedgwood plaques provided decoration not always in harmony with their setting. Some small drawing room cabinets, as plainly rectangular as any of the seventeenth century, mounted on fluted, gilded legs, were becomingly ornamented with paintings of pictorial scenes in the style of Kauffmann and Cipriani. Even on mahogany work cross-bandings and border lines in contrasting woods were frequently introduced.

The end of the century, when Sheraton was working in London, was marked by many delicate little china and bureau cabinets, often painted and inlaid with flowers and mounted on dainty tapering legs, fitted with castors. Such details as feet and glazing bars were particularly graceful. Sheraton's own designs often indicated the use of curtains behind the glass. Some bureaux and bureau-cabinets of this period had cylinder tops instead of flaps; segments of pine or mahogany were glued horizontally in a quarter-circle and veneered so that when lifted from the bottom by knobs the whole lid curved backwards into the body of the piece (Fig. 132). Additional space for writing was supplied by a slide beneath. Other bureau designs included the tambour front favoured by both Hepplewhite and Sheraton in which narrow slats of wood with rounded front edges were glued on to a fabric backing, the result being sufficiently pliable to slide in curved runners.

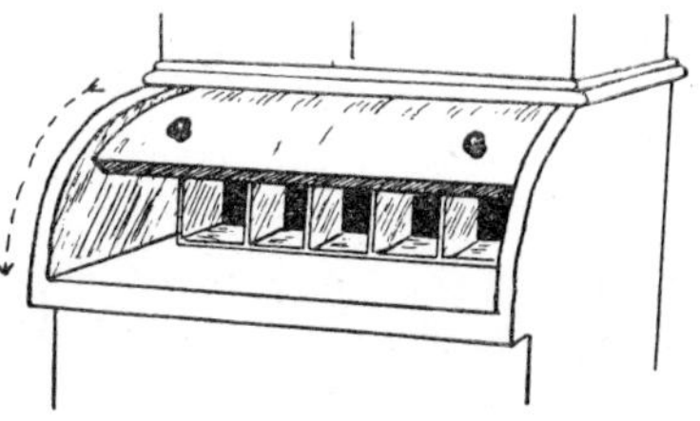

Fig. 132

A heavy cabinet at this time was sometimes mounted on turned feet instead of the earlier plinth, the drawers and now more frequent cupboard doors of the lower section being divided by attached columns, turned and carved: as with the sideboard, so with the cabinet, the turn of the century brought a demand for many heavy, rather pompous designs. Diamond glazing dated from about 1800. Sheraton appears to have taken a particular interest in study and library furniture and especially in ingenious devices such as collapsible step-ladders, disappearing book-rests and the like. But indeed this might be expected of a man who, in his first published writings, described himself not as furniture designer nor even as drawing master but as "Thomas Sheraton junior, mechanic".

13

CORNER CUPBOARDS

QUEEN Mary, wife of William III, gave encouragement to a particularly delightful fashion when she enriched Hampton Court with a magnificent collection of Oriental porcelain and delft ware. Before the end of the Stuart régime every drawing room of fashion had its display of "chiney ware", whether on open shelves, in a cabinet or in the built-in beaufait in which slender wooden pillars—sometimes a door—separated a many-shelved alcove from the rest of the panelled room.

The term "beaufait" appears to have had wide application to any type of built-in recess; indeed it would be interesting to trace the use of the word, variously spelt, to the several pieces of furniture, more or less three-cornered, from the earliest fifteenth-century three-legged stool, with which it has been associated. To the furniture collector the beaufait is important as the graciously elegant forerunner of the corner cupboard. Today, corner cupboards of all types are particularly popular antiques. During most of the eighteenth century they were customary dining room furnishings, but it may be noted as indication of their minor rôle that none of the most famous eighteenth-century trade catalogues featured them at all.

The earliest corner cupboards may date from pre-Restoration days (Charles I's inventory referred to "one little three-cornered cupboard"), but most of the oak examples which suggest the mid-seventeenth century were doubtless made much later by country workmen for provincial houses. It was only in the finely panelled room of the 1690's, dignified outcome of post-Restoration

For lacquer work in its richest form, it is necessary to turn to the cabinet, whether of Oriental workmanship or made in this country in similar style. This particularly fine example is decorated in brilliant colours, including scarlet and primrose yellow. The carved and silvered stand is English, balanced by the notable cresting to front and sides of the cabinet.

a. This bookcase in the Chippendale manner shows the swan-neck pediment and heavy "Gothic" glazing bars. Typical flush panels of beautiful Cuban mahogany.

b. The bell-hung "pagodas", fret-cresting and square construction d this mahogany piece to the m eighteenth-century "Chinese" peri

c. Like (*b*), this breakfront bureau with fret-carved gallery shows the use of mahogany astragal glazing bars. The fall-front drawer was in vogue from about 1765.

d. Dating to the late eighte century, this satin-wood bureau bo case has outward-sweeping "Fren feet continuing the curve of the sha apron.

extravagances, that the piece became established. Its Netherlands counterpart is not hard to find, stiff-flowered marquetry and the double-ogee outlines beloved of all Netherlands craftsmen being seen in many specimens probably brought to this country late in the century.

The built-in architectural "beaufait" may be dated between 1690 and 1770. By the middle of the eighteenth century two distinct types of movable cupboard had been evolved from it in this country: the simple hanging-corner cupboard may be dated 1690-1810; the approximation between this and the beaufait, a complete movable unit but of heavy construction and twice the height of the hanging cupboard, 1745-1800.

The built-in beaufait completely filled the corner or alcove from floor to ceiling, harmonizing inconspicuously with the panelled walls, stucco ceiling and ornate doorways of the period. Usually constructed of pine, sometimes of oak, it was divided into two parts, following the line of the dado moulding around the room. The upper two-thirds formed an open recess edged with curving shelves; the lower portion was more often enclosed by a panelled door. Architecturally, the principal features were the side margins flanking the opening and the finely-shaped top. The sides occasionally ran straight to the side walls but were more usually shaped in broad chamfers. These splays lent themselves to the handsome architectural effects associated with such designers as William Kent, to fluted panelling, to classical pilasters topped by carved capitals supporting the cornice, even to insertions of mirror glass to lighten a dusky corner. On such a piece the top was square, with straight, rather heavy cornice, but most frequently the open recess below was in the form of a lunette, and in simpler examples this was the principal feature of the design; it might be plain, ribbed, or carved in the semblance of a shell to form an apse supported by half-hidden fluted pilasters—a line copied from such Italian sculptors as Sansovino and adapted to many uses.

The shelves followed the lines of the back panelling, smoothly rounded or with the corner angle at the back cut off by a wide board. Finely fretted brackets supported the shelves when these were left unenclosed. By about 1700, however, it had become the fashion for all shelves to be enclosed, at first behind one long door and a little later behind separate doors to the upper and lower sections. By early in the eighteenth century the use of a pair of doors, opening in the middle, had come in, although contemporary paintings indicate that the older style continued in use.

For a short time a sheet of bevelled mirror glass, such as was produced at the famous Vauxhall glass works, was introduced on the cupboard door, the old bevels lacking the sharp regularity of modern work. But after 1730-40 mahogany panels and clear glazing were preferred.

The lower cupboard was still enclosed in panelled doors and the shelves, and occasionally drawers, in this section were consequently cut straight across the front. But in the upper section, even when the doors were panelled and not glazed, shelves with curved edges were more usual. These built-in cupboards were frequently painted to match the room, whether ivory, olive green, buff, or cool bluish-grey. In delightful contrast, some interiors were more richly coloured, in tones of red, green, yellow, and especially blue. Such features as the shell top might be picked out in gilt.

Meanwhile corner cupboards as complete, movable units were being made in two sections in the early eighteenth century, being reputed to have originated in Wales. Some London examples may be credited to the Queen Anne period made of the richly coloured lacquer-boards imported from the Orient or fronted with mirror plates. But it was in the 1740's, when heavy architectural furniture was being superseded by lighter French styles and houses with thinner walls were being built for a newly-rich clientele, even panelling giving place to wallpapers, that they began really to oust the architectural feature. They were raised off the floor by short bracket feet and no longer reached quite to the ceiling. Only their rough, unfinished backs showed that they were still intended to stand permanently in the one position.

In construction these reflected the various trends of the period. Mahogany, the perfect wood for tracery work, was now becoming established, and crown glass was being taken into general use, with the result that corner cupboards, whether two-tiered or single pieces, received light, elegant treatment: by the mid-century finely glazed single and double doors had become their most important features.

Until then, the heavy bars and rectangular outlines of the walnut period had been the rule for cabinet glazing, but the new narrow mahogany astragal bars offered the cabinet-maker infinitely greater scope for shapely curving tracery, to fit shaped pieces of glass, and in some cases augmented by carving glued to the glass itself. Thirteen or fifteen of these small panes composed the average cupboard door.

In its general outlines the two-tiered corner cupboard of this period showed the robust mid-century treatment of classic cornice with dentil course, or ornamental pediment. Such designs as the broken arch and swan-neck were particularly favoured, with a prominent central finial—urn, torch, carved shell—giving dignity to its corner setting. At this period, of course, any form of cornice still had to be built up tier by tier, to form a profile such as can be cut in one motion by a modern machine.

To the sides of the cupboard doors the broad chamfers were typically decorated with lattice work, fluted pilasters, incised carving, and were based on swelling bracket feet.

During the last quarter of the century glazed tracery became less popular, alternatives including exquisitely figured veneers in satin-wood, panels of marquetry and painted decoration as well as simple inlaid borders and motifs in native woods or panels of mahogany or oak.

Two-tier cupboards of the last years of the eighteenth century lost the distinction of the interior half-dome top, and the shelves their graceful waved outlines, although edges were sometimes gilded in the comparatively few still made with glazed doors. Narrower sides, plain, panelled, or fluted, took the place of the earlier pilasters and drawers sometimes separated the two sections. Occasionally a cupboard might show a lower section composed entirely of drawers, a vertical desk-flap fitment, or a table or desk-top which could be drawn out into the room. Some were bow-fronted, a style unsuited to a pediment, and which, even with a straight cornice, necessitated a special form of construction in small sections to keep the end grain from coming to the front on the curve. After 1810, few but heavy oak farmhouse examples were made and the scarcity of portable two-tiers to-day bears witness to the fact that they were never widely popular.

Immensely more successful in the second half of the eighteenth century was the still-less pretentious hanging corner cupboard, nailed or screwed to the wall through the back and supported to a considerable extent by the dado moulding. This cupboard was probably first introduced as a bedroom feature in place of the old livery cupboard, as a short, stumpy affair with plain, straight top, obviously designed to hang well above eye level. A few hanging corner cupboards show the oak treatment of raised panels carried out in walnut—typical of the transition period of the late seventeenth century. By 1700, however, contemporary cupid's bow panels were being executed in finely balanced burr walnut veneers bordered with strips of the straight grain. As with contemporary two-tiered examples, bevel-edged mirrors with shaped tops were sometimes introduced on the doors, soon superseded by plain sheets of wood, and the clear glazing that achieved its greatest popularity in the mid-eighteenth century.

The use of oak, walnut, fruit-woods, mahogany, and occasionally japanned pine, indicates the wide range of this cupboard's success through the eighteenth century. Examples decorated in the Oriental manner may date from the vogue around 1700; Lady Grisell Baillie paid ten shillings for one in 1715. But many are undoubtedly later, when furniture japanned and painted with Chinese motifs was again in fashion.

The elaborate fret-cut cresting above the cornice was a feature of some hanging corner cupboards made around 1750; others with flat tops were surmounted by two or three small display shelves. Not until after the middle of the century were hanging corner cupboards made in quantity, however, and their vogue then was characterized by the use of poor quality mahogany and cheaper oak with simple moulded cornice and plainly panelled doors.

a. A walnut hanging corner cupboard, door panelled with a Vauxhall plate glass mirror surrounded by half-round moulding. About 1725.

Iahogany portable corner cupboard
bow front. Late eighteenth century.

a. The early wide-bevelled Vauxhall plate mirror of the 1690's was usually framed in a broad ovolo mould topped by flat cresting. This example shows colourful marquetry in the Dutch manner.

b. Panels of seaweed marque between strips of matching ven surround this mirror which has sim marquetry in a cresting of fir carved walnut wood.

c. This wall mirror, like (*d*), is typical of the early Georgian architectural style. The figured walnut veneer is enriched with gilded gesso.

d. This ornate gilded gesso exan has egg-and-dart mouldings, gadrooning around the glass. escutcheon in the cresting and she the base are typical.

By Sheraton's day these cupboards were being made in their thousands, their double doors usually flat and panelled, occasionally bow fronted but seldom glazed. Most of these examples had flat, plainly-moulded tops or simple pear-drop arcading below the cornice mould, but a small proportion showed the hooded pediments and vase finials of the earlier years. Small drawers were sometimes fitted beneath or inside the cupboard, where dull green paint set off the porcelain arrayed on shelves which were often grooved for greater safety.

Decoration in these comparatively inexpensive little cupboards obviously depended entirely on the amount their purchasers could afford. Among the most effective were everyday examples in oak unpretentiously inlaid in native fruit-woods with borders, scrolls, or shells, reflecting the taste of their period.

14

ORNAMENTAL MIRRORS

THE beds Queen Elizabeth slept in have an air of superiority to this day. But what of the mirrors, those most intimate witnesses of Gloriana's thousand moods? How she must have hated the dark secretiveness of her own countrymen's products, turning instead to Continental work or, better still, to such gallant painters as Nicholas Hilliard of whom she commanded portraits wherein no shadow marred the royal features.

The native-made "speculum" of Elizabethan England could at best tell a poor tale of a woman's beauty. This small piece of polished metal was little better than the mirrors of silvered bronze used in Etruria and China two thousand years earlier. Such hand mirrors were made in Anglo-Saxon England and were customarily carried in the girdle in medieval days. Even Henry VIII's wardrobe at Windsor detailed "a square loking steale glasse set in blew vellet all over embrowderde with Venice golde [gold thread] and damaske pearles".

Mirror manufacture in England at this time was, indeed, far behind that of the Continent. Before the end of the twelfth century German reference was being made to a "spiegel-glas"; in 1250 the Dominican Vincent de Beauvais recorded that the best mirrors were made from glass and lead; references by such writers as Dante (1265-1321) to a "leaded mirror" indicate that glass mirrors of some size were then becoming more generally known. It would appear that throughout the thirteenth and fourteenth centuries the Venetian glass-workers tried in vain to copy the German method. There are English references to mirror glass as early as the thirteenth century, but the extreme rarity of this country's imports prior to 1660 can be judged by the fact that even in the mid-seventeenth century mirror plates of "steel"—approximately one part of tin to three parts of copper—were being imported in considerable quantities and were considered worthy of fine frames, such as tortoiseshell veneer bordered with ebony. Convex steel mirrors were in demand for kindling fires.

Glass mirrors from the Continent were fitted with more extravagant frames of silver in the contemporary French style and occasionally of colourful enamel. Others, plainly edged in olive wood, were given outer frames of lively Stuart embroidery in colourful silks and wools and in the quaint high-relief pictorial embroidery known as stump work. The fashionable demand for these mirrors in the gay post-Restoration England of Charles II can be gauged by such small items as a casket dressing case of 1668 in which the top part represented a doll's drawing room set all around with mirrors. Only such rarely favoured individuals as Nell Gwyn and the Duchess of Portsmouth could possess in reality a stateroom lined with mirror glass.

During the sixteenth century the Venetians had discovered a combination of mercury and tin with which glass could be "silvered"—a jealously guarded secret that quickly brought riches to the monopoly-holders. But it was not until late in the seventeenth century that manufacture of mirrors became established in England. Clear glass was being made in this country by 1575, and in 1615 the glass monopolist, Sir Robert Mansell, applied for a patent to make glass mirrors. By 1623, according to contemporary records quoted by H. J. Powell, five hundred glass-workers were "making, grinding, polishing and foyling looking glasses".

In 1664 a proclamation forbade the import of looking glasses, but this was withdrawn four years later. It was not until about 1675, however, that the design and manufacture of mirror frames became part of the furniture-maker's job. By this time, the important Vauxhall glass works at Lambeth, established in 1665 and owned by the Duke of Buckingham, who then held the monopoly for mirror plate, was producing mirror glass with bevelled edges in the Venetian style but, according to Evelyn in 1676, "far larger and better".

For another fifteen years or more these mirrors remained comparatively small, never longer than about forty-two inches, as large plates tended to warp and so produce irregular reflections. The process of "floating" glass plate—pouring the molten glass into shallow trays and pressing it flat—only began to be practised in France in the late seventeenth century, England following her lead. The process is described in *The Art of Glass* (1699) by H. de Blancourt. Earlier mirror glass was made by blowing the "metal" into large cylinders and splitting them open while intensely hot. This process produced sheets only about half the thickness of modern mirror glass. Their slightly rounded bevels were usually pressed into shape while the glass was semi-molten, for bevelling with the sand wheel was an early eighteenth century development. Small looking glasses, however, might have shallow, hand-ground bevels about an inch wide around their edges. A thin coating of mercury, backed with protective tinfoil, was applied to the perfectly flat and highly polished plate under a pressure which secured adhesion, and the mirror was ready for framing.

To-day these early mirror plates are usually discoloured and the backing in disrepair. A bill dated as early as 1686 recorded four days' work at Woburn Abbey which consisted of "polishing and silvering" three mirrors and repairing thirty-two looking glasses. The job was considered sufficiently important to justify the cost of two days spent each way "upon ye Roade".

Wooden frames began to be made for enclosing mirrors from about 1675. These were squarish rectangles of deal, following the lines of mid-seventeenth-century raised panelling. Their slightly convex bead or broad ovolo moulding, from three to six inches wide, offered an excellent basis for cross-grain and oyster walnut veneer and a wealth of more elaborate decoration, as befitted the new luxury.

Usually an elaborate semi-circular cresting completed the design in these late Stuart mirrors, following the lines of earlier silver models and sometimes executed in silvered wood. The usual form of cresting was a central decorative

The rococo extravagance of the d-eighteenth century was ɔressed in frames composed of olls, leafy branches, and exotic birds.

b. Many of these carved and gilded mirrors displayed the "Chinese" and "Gothic" moods of the mid-century with pillars, birds, scrolls, rocks, and waterfalls.

It was as a contrast to such extrava-nce that the gilded mirror frames of e 1770's expressed the classic style voured by the brothers Adam, with urn and acanthus carved pediment.

d. Also dating to the later eighteenth century, this gilded mirror shows decoration of composition on a wire core against a border of blue glass.

a. The swivel dressing-glass dates from the early eighteenth century. This example has a frame veneered with short strips of cross-grained walnut.

b. Veneered tables of this type might serve as dressing-tables in the late seventeenth century. The marquetry is of the scrolling arabesque variety.

motif bordered in an arch of fine piercing and fret-cut outline. This was a Venetian style; but it is interesting to note the similarity between these early frames and contemporary firebacks, then becoming heavily crested and showing similar bold, naturalistic carving in deep relief. For those who could afford them, simply-framed hanging mirrors served at this period for toilet use as well as for decorative splendour; toilet mirrors are considered in greater detail in Chapter 15.

By the end of the century the most fashionable mirrors were becoming taller, their proportions more handsome. The use of olive wood, of tortoiseshell veneer edged in ebony, and of borders of brightly coloured glass, suggest early imitation of Italian styles in mirror frames. The glass surrounds of the late seventeenth and early eighteenth centuries, framed in narrow wooden beading, were of many varieties and particularly costly, the makers usually assembling their work in the room it was to adorn. Sapphire blue was a favourite colour for such borders, cut in conventional patterns, the joints being masked by small white glass rosaces, cut and ornamented.

Verre eglomisé was the name given in the nineteenth-century to another variety of glass-decoration, after Glomy, an eighteenth-century master of the art which itself was far older, having been practised in England from the thirteenth century. In point of fact, Glomy may have done little himself beyond painting on the back of clear glass with opaque colours. But the term is more usually applied to painting backed by metal foil to achieve a highly decorative effect, entirely different from that of the later Georgian glass-picture in which a print produced the basic outlines. On mirrors framed with glass, *verre eglomisé* was highly regarded during the reigns of William III and Anne but was "old fashioned" in an advertisement of 1727.

Another variant of the craft consisted of fine linework scratched in the gilded back of the glass framing which was then closely backed by a second layer of glass. Sometimes the backing glass was coloured; black and gold, and red and gold produced particularly handsome effects on the frame and cresting of such an exotic mirror. A mirror so bordered was frequently crested with gilt gesso, the table and pair of vase or candle stands designed to accompany it being perhaps brightly japanned.

Wheel engraving on the glass borders was another expensive taste of the late Stuart period, executed almost entirely by German immigrants while it was still too rare to be applied to drinking glasses. Knots of flowers accompanied monograms and crests which indicated the individual nature of the work. Cut and engraved decoration might be featured on the mirror itself where occasionally a small painting appeared on an unsilvered portion. In 1693 Gerreit Jensen charged three hundred pounds "for 3 large pannells of all Glass with a border of rought glass round about them with carved worke upon the Glass of the middle pannell".

Mirrors in the extravagant Continental style, too large to be made in one piece, were fitted with overlapping bevels, sometimes masked by moulding. Expense was the only limit to their possibilities as luxuriously decorative architectural features, introducing gilded pilasters, pediments and similar details in the grand manner of Wren and his followers. The Grinling Gibbons school of wood carvers produced many wonderfully elaborate lime-wood frames with naturalistically portrayed birds, fruit, garlands of flowers, cherubs' heads, and urns, above, around, and often overlapping the glass. Other lavish frames of the period were of silver, chased and embossed, or of ebony with silver plaquettes. Others again caught a glint of colour in panels of marquetry work as this passed through its changing fashion phases. Accompanying tables and pairs of stands—sometimes chests of drawers—were frequently decorated to match all these types of mirror framing.

More vividly colourful were the popular Oriental lacquer boards cut to fit the mirror without regard for their pictorial work. Gay tassels and coloured cords or ribbon might be used for hanging. The application of gilded gesso to mirror frames was an obvious development when this ultra-lavish decoration was in vogue between 1700 and 1735. But, at the other extreme, mirrors without any frames—"naked glasses"—might be fitted into the panelling of a fashionable room.

The indefatigable Celia Fiennes in her diary, *Through England on a Side Saddle*, describing a visit to "Lord orfford" noted ". . . There was no Looking-glass but on ye chimney piece and just opposite in ye place a Looking-glass used to be was 4 pannells of glass in Length and 3 in breadth set together in ye wanscoate. Ye same was in another drawing roome which was for my Lord. The dineing room had this Looking-glass on ye two peers between the three windows; it was from ye top to ye bottom 2 pannells in breadth and 7 in Length so it shews from top to toe. . . ." Naturalistic carvings of the Gibbons school "all in white wood without paint or varnish" were another feature of these rooms.

Early in Anne's reign wall glasses of less exotic quality also began to lose their rather square proportions. By 1700 J. Gumley of Lambeth, for example, was using larger sheets of mirror glass, and on projecting piers of wall between tall windows it became a more general fashion to introduce the tall narrow "pier glasses" described by Celia Fiennes, still sometimes of necessity made of several pieces of mirror plate and usually harmonizing with marble-topped "pier tables" beneath. This rich fashion continued throughout the eighteenth century, the carver and gilder who worked on the joiner-made mirror frame also being responsible for the decoration of the accompanying pier or console table. The typical long room with three windows required a matching pair of these glasses.

Early frames, fairly flat and narrow, were topped with cresting in keeping with their dignified surroundings. As might be expected, many mirrors were framed in curving outline; rich carving around the base was often balanced by an architectural type of shaped or pedimented head, often following the earlier architectural style of the great Inigo Jones (1573-1652). The broken pediment of the early Georgian era offered a setting for a conspicuous finial, often a shield, plumes, or mask, finely carved in full relief. The central feature of the base was frequently a shell. A narrow gilt gesso moulding, carved with some such simple classic motif as the egg-and-tongue, bordered the glass itself. By Georgian days the mirror tended to be rather smaller than those at the beginning of the century, but the narrow sides of the frame contributed to the general impression of height.

Simpler frames of the early eighteenth century were little more than an inch wide. Strips of cross-grain walnut veneer or overlay, never more than a few inches long and much less on the curves, decorated their plain surrounds of rounded or ogee section. The bevelled glass, sometimes double-bevelled, as well as the frame was "scalloped"—shaped at the top by the glass grinder—in any of the many graceful curving forms—arc, cusp, or ogee—popular at this period. Typical was an arch flanked by cusps and ogee shaping (Fig. 133). In a similar way, mirrors were mounted in rounded section walnut bead on many Queen Anne cabinets, corner cupboards, and other display pieces, as described in previous chapters.

The first half of the eighteenth century was the age of the "chimney glass". Its three plates were set side by side across the mantelshelf, the wide flat bevels of the narrow outer plates clipping the edges of the wider central one to hold it in position, often without any attempt to mask the join, although carved mouldings, and even glass pilasters, might be introduced. The tops of all three plates often followed a flowing serpentine line, but by Georgian days the glasses of rectangular mirrors, as distinct from the frames, had lost their curved tops. The frame, one and a half to two inches wide, might be walnut, lacquer or gilt gesso, cross-banded walnut generally indicating early work. An early eighteenth century chimney-piece development was the introduction of a painting above a mirror of the rectangular "landscape" shape (its width greater than its height) within the carved and gilded frame.

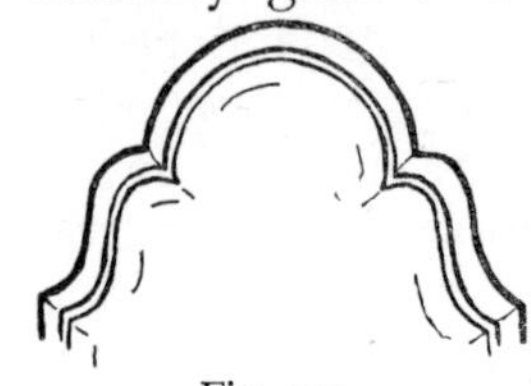

Fig. 133

In early Georgian days the pier glass, perhaps as much as seven feet tall, was an extremely imposing and important detail in the massive schemes devised by such architects as William Kent. The frame was of soft wood, usually gilded deal or lime, sometimes gilded gesso, occasionally mahogany or walnut but even then touched with gilt to emphasize the mouldings. Classic frieze and cornice, particularly the broken pediment around an elaborate finial, was balanced by base scrolls finished with a carved and shaped apron, the whole being in keeping with the scroll-laden, pedimented doorways, chimney pieces and so on favoured by such architects as Gibbs and Vanbrugh. Freer but no less elaborate designs surrounded elliptical glasses; even the popular wall barometer might be featured in the centre of an impressive mirror. In the *Daily Courant*, July 29, 1724, James Welsh advertised himself as glass-grinder and looking-glass-maker, offering "Peer, Chimney, or Sconce Glasses, fine Dressing-Glasses, Coach, Chariot, or Chair-Glasses with Plate Sash Glasses, etc. Old Glasses cleaned and made into new Fashions"—the final sentence indicating the value of mirror plate.

Plainer frames of 1720-50 depended for decoration on fine walnut veneers—burr walnut in the best—enhanced by carved gilt mouldings and an eagle or similar finial in full relief.

Technical developments in glass manufacture in 1745 assisted the natural tendency of the period towards lighter types of wall mirror, often without bevelled edges. For the next twenty years such brilliant carvers as Chippendale, whose father was noted for his mirror and picture frames, expressed an intensely rococo French style. These mirror frames, generally gilt, were carved and undercut in a restless elaboration of openwork scrolls, mingled with Gothic arches, pillars, ruins, and Chinese designs of pagodas, bells, long-beaked birds, and "waterfalls" almost unbelievably fantastic. Many credited to Chippendale, however, are certainly not his work, and it has been pointed out that about a hundred years earlier J. C. Erassmus had published somewhat similar designs in Nuremberg. A notable characteristic was a frequent avoidance of symmetry. Chippendale designs were the delight of contemporary copper plate engravers who applied them around trade cards, ball tickets, and frontispieces to books. Carving on mid-century pier glass and overmantel frames in the Chippendale style was frequently emblematical, introducing such themes as the art of music or trophies of war.

A notable minor product of the "Chinese" vogue was the

mirror plate sent to China to be painted on the back of the glass in fluid colour, in a mixture of western and eastern styles, and then silvered. Some were framed in Chinese teak.

Contemporaneously, for less expensive mirrors, typical mahogany frames of the mid-eighteenth century were narrow, resembling earlier walnut examples. Decoration was restricted to flat fret-cut designs on the top and base board. In many cases these were merely the background for a full-relief centre-piece, most usually a gilded bird with outspread wings (Fig. 134). The inner edge of the frame had a gilt fillet, and it was fashionable, round 1755, to attach the mirror to the wall with knobs decorated with painted enamels such as were produced at Battersea.

Fig. 134

When Adam began planning furniture soon after 1758 and employing such eminent makers as Chippendale to execute his designs, rococo frames for mirrors were soon entirely ousted by simple geometrical outlines based upon classic buildings and ornament. Early overmantel glasses by Adam were often shaped to a finely calculated horizontal ellipse, surrounded by carved Vitruvian scrolls. Later came rectangular frames around three or more mirrors which were partially obscured by a wealth of gilded ornament somewhat resembling wood carving but much of it moulded in composition over a wire core. In comparison with the over-enthusiasm of the more elaborate mid-century work, the most striking feature of this Adam design was the delicacy and judgment with which he introduced such classical motifs as vases, pateræ, pendant husk, and anthemium. Husks frequently decorated the narrow sides of these frames, remarkably resembling the Queen Anne and early Georgian acorn and oak leaf similarly introduced. From the early eighteenth century candle sconces had been included in the frames of many mirrors. For others, separate girandoles with branching sconces were designed in keeping with the mirrors and were themselves often backed with reflective glass.

Prices accompanying some of Adam's original mirror designs in the Soane Museum are revealing. A comparatively simple example, about six feet by four feet six inches was calculated: Glass, £10.15s.; frame, £5; painting, £1; ornament painting, £5.5s., total £22. Reduced to £21.5s.6d. But elaborate pier glasses with painted medallions and rich classical ornament might cost £120 or £160 a pair.

The mirrors of this period varied vastly in detail, but all were constructed on the same basic principles, such recorders of current fashion as the Hepplewhite firm showing work entirely in the Adam tradition.

From about 1790 a popular form of overmantel mirror consisted of three bevelled plates surrounded and divided by a narrow reeded frame and mounted on rounded feet. Characteristics included strongly-featured side pilasters supporting a hollow moulded cornice decorated with a row of gilt balls. Enrichment of these mirrors followed the current Empire styles and they continued to be made in the provinces through the nineteenth century.

Another late eighteenth century fashion was the circular convex mirror. The outer edge of the moulded circular gilt frame was reeded, sometimes banded at intervals with cross ribbons; the inner edge rimmed with a black fillet. In the hollow of these mouldings small gilt balls or rounded flowers were introduced and the finishing touch consisted of foliage supporting a gilt eagle in full relief with wings outspread. Indeed, the association of both birds—especially eagles—and their plumes with mirror decoration throughout the whole period is noteworthy. Moreover, it is often evident that many of the finials in cartouche or escutcheon form are but simplified or debased versions of either this bird motif or the Prince-of-Wales feathers favoured by even such early leaders of design as William Kent.

15

DRESSING TABLES

THE dressing table in all its glory of frills and flounces, fitted compartments and disappearing mirrors, originated in the eighteenth century. In the sixteenth century any table might be called into use; even in the seventeenth, the small, shapely tables most associated with toilet requirements served equally for writing or card playing. To the Elizabethan and early Stuart lady the important toilet accessory was her "sweet coffer" or dressing casket. In this she kept her precious cosmetics and perfumes, wrapped in the wisp of toile that first acquired the name *toilette*. Some of these caskets were extremely handsome, decorated with carved ebony, inlays of coloured woods and green-stained ivory or lavishly-embroidered cloth. Some were fitted with small and treasured Venetian glass mirrors; but imported mirrors were extremely expensive and not until nearly 1700 could English-made mirror glass begin to be regarded as much more than a royal extravagance.

As befitted their value, most seventeenth-century wall mirrors were framed for splendid display rather than with any thought for practical toilet use. Mirrors specifically designed for the dressing table, like the table itself, were early-eighteenth-century developments.

The typical small, all-purpose oak table of the seventeenth century had a thin top measuring perhaps three feet by two, mounted on simple turned legs. Frequently one or two drawers were let into the frieze, those before 1660 distinguishable by their grooves fitting into projecting side-runners in the table framework. After the Restoration, French and Dutch influence revolutionized English furni-

a. As in the previous example, this early Georgian toilet mirror has the bevelled plate shaped at the top, crossbanded frame, and finely constructed drawers in concave and convex curves.

b. An oak dressing-table of William III's reign, with finely shaped frieze edged with beading. The drawer is set immediately below the thin table top.

a. By the 1760's the mahogany toilet mirror might have fret-cut, flat cresting. The glass was square-cut at the top, and the drawers mainly vertical with only concave shaping.

b. Indicative of the Continental styles introduced during the reign of William III is this walnut side or dressing table. The mould edging the top is finely carved.

ture styles, but for many years these little tables showed only such minor advances as twist-turned legs linked by flat stretchers placed diagonally. Examples were made in both oak and the newly-fashionable walnut in which the deep, waved frieze included a rounded kneehole flanked by two tiny drawers with pear-drop handles; only the absence of leather glued to the tops distinguished them from contemporary writing tables.

Many of these tables had the swelling "Portuguese" legs which, with flat, waved stretchers, dated from the last years of the seventeenth century. But by then another and far more commodious piece of bedroom furniture was becoming established—the chest of drawers. A wall mirror framed in marquetry work suspended above a chest of drawers similarly decorated on top and drawer fronts, was as handsome an outfit as any great lady could require. As early as 1705 Christopher Thornton, Southwark mirror dealer, appears to have made a feature of selling chests of drawers—and no other furniture—at his mirror shop, *The Looking Glass*.

Nothing could be in greater contrast, however, to the particularly slender design of the early single-purpose dressing table in finely matched walnut veneers with its essentially feminine, almost fragile air. Queen Anne and early Georgian examples followed plain lines that are especially appealing to-day. Two or three drawers above and around the kneehole constituted the only fitment; a shell carved on each cabriole knee, above slim leg and plain pad foot, most usually the only ornament.

Standing on the table or suspended above it might be one of the new Vauxhall plate mirrors described in the previous chapter, with its thin plate and flat, blunt-edged bevels. This mirror might be as much as eighteen inches high and twelve inches wide, framed in a convex section bead or simple ogee mould built up of short pieces of cross-grain walnut laid over a deal foundation. Often a gilt fillet separated glass and frame, both of which, in early work, were usually shaped at the top in graceful curves and frequently crowned with arched fret-cut cresting.

As yet dressing table and toilet mirror were developing as independent units. The immediate mirror improvement consisted of the Continental idea of mounting the glass on uprights by means of a swivel fitment so that it could be tilted to any angle. Screw action movements were used to attach the mirror, slightly above half height, to a pair of slender supports, raking backwards a little and either plain, turned or fluted, their finials nearly as tall as the glass itself. Such uprights required a solid base, and for the purpose a charming miniature bureau or nest of drawers was devised, made of deal and veneered or japanned to match the mirror frame. Most usually this base was built up in one, two or three receding tiers each consisting of one or more tiny drawers, their fronts most usually shaped in concave curves, often both vertically and horizontally, their minute pulls of brass, their interiors neatly lined with oak, black walnut, or, later, mahogany. Small feet, most usually bracket shaped and often set beneath splayed corners, with or without a narrow plinth, raised the little piece an inch or so above the dressing table (Fig. 135). "Some Japan'd Swing Glasses" were advertised in *The Spectator* in 1711.

In more elaborate examples the bureau idea—apparently never far from the mind of the ladies' dressing table designer—was carried further. A slanting flap covered the tiers of drawers and intervening pigeon holes; this opened on to pull-out bearers fitted at the sides of an additional drawer in the base. From such a design it was no great step to the first complete dressing table unit, a bureau of this type, still small but twice the width of the mirror itself, standing not upon a separate dressing table but upon its own slender legs. Early eighteenth-century examples, some no doubt brought over from the Continent, are to be found richly veneered in exotic woods. Others were made from Oriental lacquer boards, not to be confused with the popular contemporary japanning executed in England and often by amateurs.

Fig. 135

To-day, many Queen Anne dressing tables seem impossibly small and fragile; indeed most early designers of them appear to have been obsessed with the femininity of their patrons. More robust, though sometimes extravagant, were the designs of Chippendale and his contemporaries around the mid-eighteenth century. It was not until after 1750 that walnut lost its vogue for bedroom furniture, and even when mahogany began to take its place many dressing tables were still made in the earlier style with graceful cabriole legs. Innumerable others were of the simple pedestal design, of which many heavier, mahogany examples were produced for the Georgian dandy.

Often such a dressing table might be better described as a chest of drawers fitted with a knee recess. The recess was flanked from floor upwards by deep drawers, three to five each side and with a special drawer above the knee hole fitted with a collapsible mirror and reading stand. Thus, when closed, the purpose of the piece might pass undetected. Others, when closed, appeared to be no more than tables with deep decorative friezes. In these the table top opened outwards from the middle to form trays flanking a mirror surrounded by numerous fitted compartments. A touch of a spring catch raised the mirror. This, too, was in keeping with the demand that dressing tables should resemble writing tables and drawing room commodes, reflecting the Georgian fashion for receiving guests while completing the toilet, and for breakfasting, alone or in company, in the bedroom.

Shaving tables were for the man of the house. For his lady, the design still had to be small and graceful, but already in Chippendale's day the vogue had begun for drawers fitted with "all conveniences for dressing". Chippendale's *Director* recorded both the plain-topped commode style and the more ambitious mirrored dressing table. For the latter, it suggested ornate shaped mirrors, flanked by mirror-fronted cupboards and topped by cherubs which in an elaborate example were placed so as to surround the mirror with silken damask draperies fringed and tasselled in gold. A "petticoat" of damask might be introduced all around the table. Burnished gold or japan work tricked out the many decorative details. Even on the comparatively simple dressing commode Chippendale recommended a wealth of brass ornament and a combination of serpentine front and swelling profile, curving frieze and scroll or knurl feet in the fashionable French manner.

It cannot be stressed too often, however, that the name of Chippendale has too easily been applied to work typical of many mid-century craftsmen. This included many comparatively simple commodes in which glowing mahogany was lightly ornamented with curved or applied fret-cut ornament around the cornice frieze and down the canted front edges. Moreover, it must be remembered that Chippendale himself produced his principal work later in the century in the classical Adam style.

The other eighteenth-century names associated especially with bedroom furniture are those of George Hepplewhite and Thomas Shearer. They recorded the fashions of the period around 1780, under the influence of Adam but aiming, as Hepplewhite put it, "to unite beauty with utility" in more every-day furniture. Both favoured dressing tables reproducing many of the earlier fittings such as collapsible mirrors inside table or commode drawers. Hepplewhite claimed, indeed, that he had devised the most complete dressing table ever made, but his typical commode dressing chests were simple bow or serpentine fronted designs. Some had reeded edges, slender tapering square legs, and spade feet. Others depended for decoration upon shaped apron and outward curving stump feet, associated with inlaid or painted ornament of flowers, ribbons, or husks.

Dressing tables at this period might bear considerable resemblance to the fitted sideboards which were developed in the late 1760's. Often they had the same rather heavy flanking pedestal cupboards—in their case usually enclosing drawers—the same arched central recess under the wide frieze drawers, and additional small cupboards above the table top in place of the sideboard urns or knife boxes.

During the middle years of the century plain mahogany was in favour but by the last quarter of the century it was rivalled by the lighter tones of satin-wood, with chestnut as a cheaper alternative. Fine pieces might be of mahogany veneered in exotic kingwood and further ornamented with marquetry in various other woods; cheaper examples were more often of painted pine.

The mirror was the most important feature of dressing table design, but the demand continued through the century for toilet glasses in combination with plainer chests of drawers and commodes not fitted with their own folding mirrors. From the earliest Queen Anne styles developed many extremely delectable little glasses, the lines of typically English designs showing less elaborate curves than those strongly influenced if not actually manufactured by the Dutch.

Fig. 136

By the mid-century, when mahogany was becoming available for bedroom furniture, the typical narrow moulded frame, separated by a gilt fillet from the wide bevelled glass, resembled the simplest wall mirror of the day. Its only shaping consisted of inward pointing corners at the top; sometimes the top had the same flat fret-cut cresting as contemporary wall mirrors. Tapering moulded uprights supported the mirror and were mounted on a veneered box base containing a single row of shaped drawers on tiny bracket feet. Screw mirror fitments were of brass and the uprights topped with tall turned finials (Fig. 136).

Mahogany toilet mirrors later in the century took on a greater variety of shapes—the shields of "Hepplewhite" chairs, upright and horizontal ellipses, and other curving forms. The flat, very narrow frames were of cross-banded veneer upon a basis of pine; rounded shapes were on some such pliant wood as yew. In the last quarter of the century some of these glasses were veneered in satin-wood on an oak base, some having painted decoration. A charming feature was the graceful curve of the supports to fit and elaborate upon the mirror outline. The small veneered boxes of drawers beneath followed bow or serpentine lines but now had vertical rather than concave fronts. Drawer handles, key escutcheons, and urn finials on the uprights were of ivory or bone. Less expensive examples were rectangular and from about 1800 this

Fig. 137

shape was particularly favoured (Fig. 137). Often convex section framing around the mirror harmonized with well-proportioned turned uprights.

Contemporary with all these styles was the cheval glass in which the uprights terminated not in a box base but in outward-curving trestle legs linked by a gracefully shaped and often inlaid stretcher (Fig. 138).

It was Sheraton, however, who devoted himself most enthusiastically to the design of cheval glasses—horse glasses as he called them—as also to dressing tables and many another remarkable piece of fitted all-purpose bedroom furniture. His tall cheval glasses were sometimes fitted with weighted height-adjustment devices: Shearer, in his *Cabinet Maker's London Book of Prices*, estimated for a screen dressing glass frame "the inside of the glass two feet six inches long, one foot six inches wide, the back fram'd with four flat panels, the weights cut by the plumber, claws, and common castors, £1 1s. 0d. If made to swing, and not to rise, 6s. less". Such glasses might be fitted with branching arms for candles, with brackets for nests of drawers, or even with fold-up fittings both for toilet and for writing.

Fig. 138

Sheraton's commode and cabinet dressing tables might combine the duties of wash-stand, with tiny basin and lead-lined drawer to receive the dirty water, and of writing table with fittings for ink and sand.

He devoted a wealth of ingenuity to devising improvements on the elaborate examples set by Hepplewhite and others so that a multitude of aids to dressing might be hidden away behind a front which was often dignified and imposing, however deplorable the occasional sham drawers and the representations of draperies painted upon glass-fronted cupboard doors. Slightly ludicrous as some designs might appear, they did not quite lose the grace and delicacy associated with Sheraton. The rounded horizontal curves, the square tapering legs and discreet use of "petticoat" hangings must have justified at the time his claim for their "elegance". Sheraton intended his work principally for mahogany and satin-wood; some satin-wood dressing tables of this period were delicately painted with classic scenes in the Italian manner.

Sheraton's early nineteenth-century work, reflecting the heavy and rather prosaic trends of the period, is attractive only in its simplest examples. More elaborate dressing tables showed a wealth of finicky ornament, and even the legs lost their tapering grace in heavier turned work.

Here again it must be emphasized that Sheraton was but one designer among many. Equally typical of the end of the eighteenth century is the well-proportioned, often bow-fronted dressing table resembling a commode. Cupboard doors flanked the rounded knee recess and the top was slotted at the back to enclose a mirror which could thus disappear discreetly into the chest when not required. Of simply painted wood, decorated with ribbons and flowers of its period, such a piece would do credit to any unknown furniture maker of the day. The same can be said, too, of the excellent workmanship in many a plainly handsome mahogany chest of drawers topped with a mahogany-framed toilet glass, the design of which was too entirely simple and direct to be worth recording at the time.

16

TRIPOD FURNITURE

"PILLAR-AND-CLAW" or tripod furniture made a notable contribution to the gracious elegance of the mid-eighteenth-century drawing room. It must be appreciated, however, that it was by no means confined to that period or even that century. Indeed, the British Museum's eleventh-century Cotton Manuscript illustrates a little round table on a central pillar above a spreading base. And innumerable tripod tables were made in the nineteenth century.

It was soon after the Restoration, however, that the design began to play an important part in English fashions not for tables but for candle stands. One of the practical furniture fashions that marked the return of Charles II and his court with new ideas from the Continent was the bedroom arrangement of a little table under a hanging wall mirror, flanked by two of these stands.

Just as the dressing tables themselves at this period were graceful but still distinctly plain little pieces, so the accompanying tripod candle stands consisted of no more than small round or many-sided trays mounted on slender turned pillars based on out-jutting, nearly horizontal feet. The majority were in walnut, but by the end of the century lacquer was also in vogue. Twist-turning, rising out of a baluster base, was frequently applied to the pillar, matched to the typical twist-turned legs of the bedroom table. The three feet dovetailed into this base followed more or less the S-scroll outline associated with this period; in William's reign the S-scrolls in claw furniture were often decidedly angular, in square section and with a definite shoulder or corner to mark the meeting of concave and convex

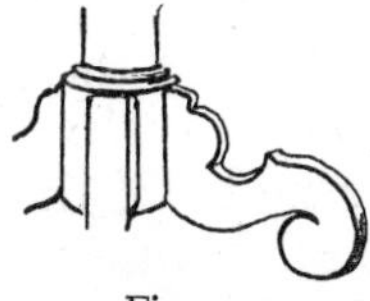
Fig. 139

curves (Fig. 139). By Anne's reign the curves were more flowing, leading naturally to the perfection of line found in the early Georgian round-section cabriole or ogee legs poised on virile paw or somewhat later ball-and-claw feet.

Even before the end of the seventeenth century, however, mirrors were developing an entirely new character as massive Vauxhall plates brought a glassy brilliance to fashionable drawing rooms—never more charming than when reflecting the mellow light of many candles. Bedroom convenience became drawing room elegance: pier glass and pier table were flanked by candle or vase stands executed in the grand manner, the pillar-and-claw outline heavily carved and lavishly gilded.

These tripod stands lent themselves particularly to the rococo extravagances of the 1750's. Chippendale's *Director* showed exceedingly lavish designs to hold candles or decorative busts. The tray was small, with shapely raised edge, the main pillar often being replaced by a group of slender uprights linked by filigree detail, giving emphasis to a "shoulder" a little below the top. This line was widely exploited at this period, being found, for instance, in the silesian and inverted-baluster stems of salvers, sweetmeat dishes, and other glass tableware. Inside one of these stands or "terms" Chippendale suggested a line-and-pulley arrangement for raising the candle as it burnt lower. Some stands sacrificed grace for safety, however, the scrolling tripod base being disproportionately large and widely splayed or else so shaped as to produce a "pigeon-toed" effect.

Gothic and Chinese motifs were exploited to the full on all these stands, some of which had tiny fretted galleries around their tops. Equally elaborate, if more dignified, were the classic designs that followed in the 1760's. The principal constructional change was the greater use of a solid plinth base from which the three slender legs rose in unbroken curves to the massive top. Vases, urns, rams' heads, and other Adam motifs contributed to the rich elaboration that crowned these stands and thus achieved more balanced compositions than were to be found earlier in the century. Fine examples might be carved in low relief all down their slender legs.

This long tapering tripod line was used for many of the tiny wash-basin stands of the late eighteenth century—where Chippendale had suggested "Gothic" pillars and arches—but Hepplewhite's adjustable reading stands returned to plainer turned and fluted pillar designs: the claw legs had lost the animal "spring" of the earlier cabriole and were more or less serpentine. Sheraton tripods defy classification: he applied the pillar-and-claw technique to a wide range of furniture, from library tables and dumb waiters to ladies' work boxes, frequently preferring four claws to three. His candle stands included designs reminiscent of Adam work, with three slender pillars rising from a solid plinth, itself mounted on three lightly-carved feet. Much of their decorative scrollwork was of composition on wire cores and thus less flimsy than it appeared. For these stands a gilded finish was still the rule, but Sheraton suggested that "in inferior drawing-rooms" they might be japanned to suit the other furniture.

The pillar-and-claw construction at its most delightful and distinguished, however, is to be found in the little "snap" tables of Georgian days. Strangely, Chippendale, who has even been credited with their invention, does not show them in his 1754 *Director*: already, then, their heyday was over. They were known in walnut and japanning, however, before the end of the seventeenth century, and in 1733, for example, the furniture belonging to Sir William Stanhope included "a mahogany scollop'd Tea-Table on a claw". By this date mahogany was only beginning to become widely used but these tables were especially a mahogany fashion, the great girth of the trees making it easy to shape the table top from a single piece of the dark, glossy wood. The large-boled "black" Virginia walnut was similarly used and may be difficult to distinguish from mahogany. Cheap work for coffee houses and public gardens was made of oak, beech, or elm.

Hogarth's *Marriage à la Mode*, Scene II (1745) shows one of these tables with the early angular S-scroll feet; and Ince

At the beginning of the eighteenth century, when in England a swivel mirror was still a rarity, many delightful small japanned examples were brought over from Holland. This one is of the most elaborate bureau type. The desk front opens on to small bearers and there is a candle slide at the side.

a. This well-balanced octagonal china table retains the vigorous ball-and-claw feet of the early Georgian period.

b. This tripod stand for a vase bust, such as Chippendale il trated in his *Director*, is notable gracious proportions and w poised legs on knurl feet.

c. Superbly carved, this octagonal example shows the pillar-and-claw table at its best. The "birdcage" is visible under the top: this portion can be lifted off the pillar when the vertical wedge is withdrawn.

d. This table has the more wide scrolling legs of the later eighteen century. The straight pillar is mo usual than the open carving of t previous example.

and Mayhew in their *Universal System of Household Furniture*, issued in parts, 1759-63, show "Three very neat designs for Claw Tables", in the rococo style of the period.

The typical early Georgian construction showed either a shapely baluster outline or else a straight-fluted column rising from a bulb shape carved with gadrooning or acanthus leaf. Dovetailed into the base of this were the three projecting claws in cabriole outline, ending in ball-and-claw (Fig. 140), hoof, or lion's paw feet. Mid-century claw variations included the French dolphin design also used by Chippendale for candle stands, and the scroll toe. Some pillars were spirally fluted; some formed of three S-scrolls suggestive of flying buttresses, giving particularly delightful play of convex and concave curves; many of the finest were richly, vigorously carved throughout their length.

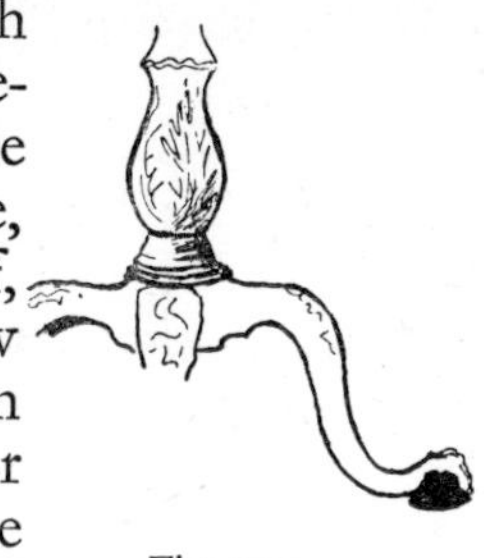

Fig. 140

Indeed, some of these tables were lavishly carved on their tops, too, for eighteenth-century craftsmen were quick to appreciate that the table's air of distinction principally depended upon the perfect shaping of the top and the impression of poise in the "claw". Simple tops might be plainly circular or shaped in a series of deep scallops, the surface sunk slightly below a moulded tray edge. More elaborate was the "pie crust" top in which the raised and moulded edge, perhaps three-quarters of an inch wide, was shaped in a series of sharp curves and points (Fig. 141): in elaborate examples the shaping might be emphasized with floral carving in low relief.

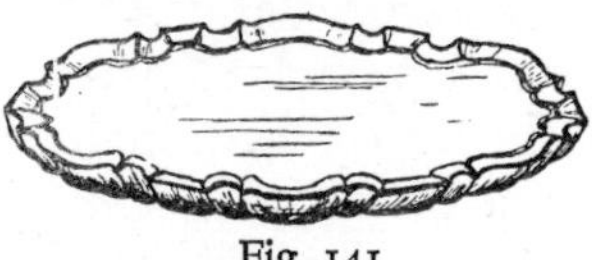

Fig. 141

Rather later came the tops of various shapes intended for china display, and edged with tiny galleries. These galleries were composed of either spindles or fret-cut tracery such as was to be found on many mahogany china tables, candle stands and other furniture, the frets being built up of three layers of wood, glued together in different ways of the grain. Later—in the 1770's—came tables enhanced with central inlay or marquetry decoration, displayed to advantage when the hinged top was tipped up, both to save space and to serve as a firescreen. Many of these tables were thus hinged; hence their name "snap tables". The top was equipped underneath with two small cross-bearers and a brass spring catch which fitted into a square socket when the table was horizontal. More elaborate was the little square platform with four tiny turned spindles supporting the top, known as a birdcage; when a wedge was pulled out the whole top lifted off.

Late in the century these tables lost much of their distinction, although many showed plain, well-turned baluster pillars. The legs tended to sprawl; in place of the cabriole the 1780's saw many concave curves with reeded moulding on more or less round feet. Late work often introduced a little pointed pendant finial under the pillar, a feature of some Queen Anne furniture. These tables became popular again in the early nineteenth century.

Accompanying and often matching these tea tables, other lower tripod stands were sometimes brought into use. These held the kettles and caddies that played an important rôle in the charming ceremonies associated with eighteenth-century tea-drinking. For example, a kettle stand with a fine baluster outline is shown in Hogarth's picture *A Musical Party*. The teapoy, consisting of a tea caddy mounted on the pillar-and-claw construction, was a nineteenth-century development.

Snap tables were not the only devices for screening eighteenth-century beauties from the great fires that warmed their lofty apartments. In the *Marriage à la Mode* scene already mentioned a large pole screen is in view, and after about 1740 the pole screen based on pillar-and-claw construction replaced to a considerable extent the various trestle and folding designs of earlier times.

Chippendale's simple designs showed shapely poles, reminiscent of his bed pillars, with well-proportioned baluster shaping immediately above cabriole legs lightly carved with acanthus foliage. His more elaborate work, like his drawing room candle stands, showed a wealth of rococo C-curves and ornate filigree work typical of his

French style. The screen itself was approximately rectangular, the narrow frame often carved and the centre piece worked in *petit point* embroidery. In 1763 William Vile supplied "For the Queen's use a neat mahogany piller and claws screen, neatly carv'd, to her Majesty's piece of Needlework, for £3 10s." During the second half of the century other forms of embroidery were more largely used. Horace Walpole refers to "a screen worked in chenille, to suit with the chimney, by the Countess of Ailesbury", and occasionally the decoration was painted on wood and backed with pleated silk.

Fig. 142

In the late years of the century the screens themselves were much smaller and more variously shaped—in ellipses, shields, and the indented outlines seen in many formalized "fan" motifs of the period. Some, framing fine prints of embroidery on satin, were glazed.

Hepplewhite often used a solid plinth base instead of the claw design, but Sheraton devised a number of screens on particularly slender concave- or convex-curving claw legs raised on long, pointed feet (Fig. 142). He intended the poles, square in section, to be bored for pulley-and-line mechanism, but more usually these screens were adjusted on their turned poles by means of metal rings controlled by spring or screw fittings.

17

LONG CASE CLOCKS

FOR the collector of old clocks there is particular interest in the National Portrait Gallery picture of Sir Thomas More and his family. This was painted for his grandson by an unknown artist in 1593, and background details include an early example of a lantern clock. This typical household wall clock of the following century with decorative brass case and dangling weights, was impracticable because inadequately protected from dust. But the interesting feature of the More clock is that it appears to have been placed in a glazed case. As early as 1542 Henry VIII had an iron clock "with a case of glasse". From such early experiments developed two types of post-Restoration clock with the mechanism wholly enclosed. One was the portable mantel clock, worked on the coiled-spring mechanism, particularly popular in the early eighteenth century. The other was the long case or grandfather which alone can be regarded as a piece of furniture.

The case of this clock was fine cabinet work, but in considering the narrow range of design during any given period it must be remembered that clock-case construction was a distinct branch of joinery; indeed, by the eighteenth century even the making of clock dials was recognized as a specific trade, involving a variety of processes. Over such a limited number of specialist craftsmen the Clockmakers' Company—granted a charter by Charles I in 1631—was able to exert some influence, although some early cases were imported.

The earliest English makers of long case clock movements were extremely highly regarded: Thomas Tompion

(1639-1713) and his pupil-nephew George Graham were buried in Westminster Abbey. Many clocks bear the makers' names, including such famous contemporaries of Tompion as Joseph Knibb and Daniel Quare: libraries can frequently supply details of these old craftsmen. Forgeries were common even in the earliest days, however, and it was because so much inferior work had been sold under the leading names, both in England and abroad, that in 1698 an Act of Parliament required every clock to be signed with the maker's "Name and Place of Abode or Freedom". But even when the maker is unknown many a clock can be dated with considerable precision—from the basic materials employed, the general outlines of the case, and various details in the dial.

Although the long case clock can be traced in England to about 1660 and may be regarded as an English development, the makers of the earliest cases were under the influence of architectural Continental work and, as a result, from the first the case was in the imported medium of flat veneer, marquetry, or lacquer, entirely dissociated from the traditional English application of carving and inlay.

Oak was used as the carcase wood, but at this period the long case clock was a luxury article: cheaply-finished oak clocks were later eighteenth-century products. On the early work the oak was covered with veneers, at first of ebony and then of walnut, fruit-woods, or yew, varied with shaped panels of flowery marquetry in the naturalistic early Dutch manner. Mahogany played no considerable part in clock-case manufacture until the second half of the eighteenth century, and then it reflected new traditions in design.

In its general outlines the seventeenth-century grandfather clock case was slender-waisted and seldom much more than seven feet tall. Its three parts consisted of a more or less square hood containing the dial and mechanism; a long narrow body for the passage of the weights, which quickly became much wider when it had to accommodate the pendulum as the longer type was introduced; and a squarish base, balancing the hood, into which the weights travelled.

The early hood was a comparatively simple structure. Until the beginning of the Hanoverian period it was almost invariably square, the straight cornice showing the strongly-projecting mould associated with all tall contemporary furniture. Until about 1695 the moulding was most usually in convex profile; later there was increasing use of deep cavetto lines. Immediately below, at front and sides, a fret-cut frieze was often introduced, to let out the chimes.

Frequently, this hood was surmounted by arched cresting sometimes carved in the cupid-and-scroll designs of contemporary chairbacks. Even by 1700, taller rooms were creating a need for taller grandfathers and an alternative solution during this transition period—particularly 1700-1705—was the addition of a flattened dome on top of the usual straight cornice. This was frequently finished with tall finials of brass or gilded wood, at the front corners and on the centre of the flat top—a style used in bracket clocks and indeed suggestive of much contemporary cabinet work. Balanced veneers, japanning, or a marquetry motif on the front of the dome linked it with dial framing, body door, and base panel similarly decorated.

Flanking the square frame to the dial glass were two columns, usually matched by two pilasters at the rear. In early work these frequently reflected the craze for tapering twist turns, occasionally following opposite twists for greater symmetry. But even before 1700 plain turned pillars were becoming more usual, capped and based with brass and sometimes even decorated with marquetry or japan-work motifs.

At this period the hood often lacked a door and had to be drawn off the clock for winding, released by a catch inside the body. This was a common feature in cheap work which, with a thirty-hour mechanism, had to be wound every day. Both these traits long persisted in country clocks. The earliest hood glazing was a square measuring only eight to nine inches; by the 1680's it might be ten inches to harmonize with an increasing width of body; further increases to eleven inches and then to twelve marked the late years of the century, and by 1720 the still larger arched dial had become established.

Until the mid-eighteenth century the dial itself was almost invariably of brass, on to which were attached the silvered ring marking the hours and the decorative brass spandrels that filled the corners. The central area of the earliest form of dial was engraved in the Dutch manner with flowers and scrolls, still to be found in cheaper work of the late seventeenth century. But this interfered with clarity and in clocks of better quality the dial was given a matted finish with fine, even punching. R. W. Symonds has pointed out that this was apparently an English innovation, providing a perfect background to the blue steel hands. The Dutch used dark velvet behind gilded hands. Joseph Knibb favoured a dial in which even the hour ring was partly cut away so that the numerals and half-hour divisions were silhouetted against the matted brass background.

This silvered hour circle, its engraved Roman numerals filled in with black wax, was small in early clocks; as the dial grew larger the ring broadened proportionately and for cheapness was made of silvered brass. Each detail of its engraving was important. Frequently a clock had only one hand, and until about 1730 the inner rim of the ring was marked with quarter-hour and half-hour divisions; until about 1760 it was usual to mark each half-hour division with a fine line extending between the hour numerals as a decorative fleur-de-lys or similar motif, although such leaders as George Graham had long banished this early notion.

The lack of a minute hand is no assurance of age, however, for much of the cheaper eighteenth-century work continued in the older tradition, whereas many London clocks were equipped with minute hands in the 1680's. While the hour hand reached precisely to the inner rim of the hour ring, the minute hand pointed as exactly to an additional outer rim engraved with minute divisions and with the Arabic figures 5, 10, 15, and so on. Tompion, always determined to achieve clarity, was the first to enlarge the hour ring: the last development was the separation of minute divisions and five-minute numerals into two circles around the circumference of the hour ring, the numerals thereupon tending to become disproportionately large.

The hour hand was always much more elaborate than the minute hand, the pierced design—double loop in many

Charles II examples—assuming somewhat the same outline as the half-hour motifs. The minute hand had little ornament except slight scrolling near the centre. Hands were particularly ornate on some early japanned clocks—just as intricate hinges and lock plates were characteristic of japanned and lacquered cabinets.

Few long case clocks were produced before 1675, when the thirty-nine inch "Royal" pendulum was made practicable for the enclosed design by Dr. Robert Hooke's anchor escapement invention. This pendulum measured a full second with its beat and made possible the separate "seconds" circle on many a clock dial below the figure XII. The seconds hand was without a tail until the mid-eighteenth century. On a few clocks the seconds dial was marked with only forty-eight divisions, each representing one and a quarter seconds: this was to accord with the clock's extra long pendulum, approximately sixty-one inches, which had a one-and-a-quarter seconds swing.

Another feature dating from Charles II's reign was a small round or square aperture showing the day of the month. This might be placed immediately above the figure VI or instead of the seconds circle under the XII. A few of these calendars were made self-adjusting to the irregular numbers of days in the months.

Occasionally a clock was made which recorded not only the mean time but also the solar time. On other clocks printed tables of "the equation of days" were pasted inside the body work, indicating how many minutes should be added or subtracted to calculate solar time from the mean time and thus be able to check the clock's timekeeping by the sun.

By 1700, too, the larger hour circle in the twelve-inch dial was balanced but not enhanced by more conspicuous treatment of the date aperture and the two holes in the dial for the winding key, now edged with burnished metal. In some clocks tiny covers over the winding holes were fitted to interior spring mechanism known as bolt-and-shutter movements: when the winding key was inserted this mechanism would be set in action and keep the clock going while the weights were being raised. This practice was

This late - seventeenth - century
ock with works by Henry Jones
s a square dial and square-headed
dy door. The key holes are
brightly ringed.

b. J. Clowes of Covent Garden made the works of this clock about 1705. The case shows seaweed marquetry and the plain-turned pillars have brass caps and bases.

a. A clock by John Simpson about 1725, in a case of figured walnut. Both face and body have arched and shouldered doors and the high dome is typical of the period.

b. The carved mahogany case of th clock by Monk of Prescot shows th ornate treatment of the later eighteent century with pillars flanking the bod door and raised panel effects on the bas

soon discontinued except for special regulator clocks.

The most important decoration of the dial, however, was lavished on the brass corner spandrels. On an engraved dial these usually received similar treatment, but for the typical matted dial they were cast separately and attached; there were some transitional variations of treatment.

Reflecting the Continental fashion, the earliest design for these chased mounts consisted of a cupid or cherub head between curved wings, but the clear-cut early work soon deteriorated into over-elaborate scrolling designs. These often enclosed the popular Restoration motif of two amorini supporting the crown, but by 1700 the scrolls tended to smother the central motif—often a female mask, such as appeared on many a gilded mirror frame in the grand manner of the period.

The only other requirement of the dial was the maker's name. At first this appeared along the base of the plate below the hour circle. By 1700 it was being introduced either on both sides of the numeral VI or else in a plaque, attached or engraved, immediately below the centre of the dial. When, early in George I's reign, the arch was added to the dial, it often housed a circular name plaque.

This development in the shape of the dial was perhaps notable rather than desirable. The trouble was that the square dial had tended to become cluttered with "improvements"—larger numerals, touches of engraving around the various details, broad burnished rings marking the winding holes, and so on. Even by 1709 Tompion was experimenting with the arched dial and by 1720 it was becoming generally accepted in fashionable lofty rooms. Early arches tended to be less than semi-circles.

By then the long case clock had lost much of the grace that characterized the earliest examples, but continued to be well-proportioned and shapely. The body continued proportionately narrower than the hood and base and the mouldings that linked the three parts were invariably neat, that under the hood being generally convex until about 1700 and thereafter more generally concave. Not until after about 1705 was the upper mould applied in reverse to the lower angle between body and base.

The front of the body was wholly dominated by the door which followed the line of the hood glazing in changing from square top to shouldered arch. In early work the door was edged in the typical contemporary manner with a projecting half-round beading, most frequently of cross-grain walnut veneer. A fashion associated with the early square door was a round or elliptical "bob glass" of greenish bull's eye glass let into it rather below half height for viewing the pendulum.

The base received inconspicuous treatment to harmonize, its front most usually given a flat panel effect, whether of japanning, of marquetry within a tiny marquetry border, or of walnut veneer with or without an edging of walnut cross-grain. The base was mounted on a slightly projecting plinth, usually plain but occasionally showing the several tiers of moulding more associated with Georgian work and occasionally low corner bracket feet and shaped apron.

The old traditions in long case clock design lingered on into the reigns of George I and George II. Walnut was still the usual veneer, although by 1715 even the last, "seaweed" variety of scrolling and comparatively colourless marquetry was being replaced by the simpler decorative medium of English lacquer or japanning. By the 1730's this had largely lost favour among the leaders of furniture fashion, but on cheaper work, good, bad, and indifferent japan, decorated with colours and gilt in a more or less Oriental manner, appeared throughout this period—the English work having a style of its own, distinct from both the exquisite Oriental products and the Dutch imitations. It must be emphasized that even on long case clocks this was essentially a cheap treatment and the backgrounds—black, red, green, blue, yellow, or cream—are seldom found to-day in good condition.

This was a period when bracket clocks were popular and rather less attention was given to the long case variety. The hood, usually following the shouldered arch outline, reflected the current fashion for variously arched cornices and very deep cavetto mouldings. Some were in elaborate outline with three tall finials, and towards the mid-century broken pediments were widely used. The shoulder-arched door was edged with ovolo moulding and fitted with plain butt hinges so that its opening was now independent of the corner pillars. These were turned and often fluted with brass bases and Doric or Corinthian capitals.

The main change in the dial was the additional brass decoration in the arch, to harmonize with the spandrels, a common design consisting of a pair of dolphins in scroll-work. This arch was variously used to house the seconds dial, a strike-silent mechanism—sometimes incorporating the maker's name—or a raised name plate which alternatively found its place lower in the dial, sometimes arching over the date aperture.

By 1730 the maker's ingenuity had produced mechanical figures to fill the arch. The first were moons moving among clouds to depict the moon's phases; by the 1750's Thomas Ogden of Halifax had made such a name for clocks with rotating moons that these became known as Halifax clocks. But by 1750 many other devices were to be found, in the arch and lower on the dial.

The body of the early Georgian clock showed the shouldered arch to the door and decorative treatment of the spandrels flanking this arch. By George II's reign the bob glass had been discontinued and the door was edged with ovolo moulding. The base tended to show slightly heavier treatment: around the mid-century a raised panel edged with moulding in the shape of a square with clipped corners frequently decorated its front.

For costly early Georgian furniture mahogany was already beginning to become established, but not until the mid-century did the fine veneers of this wood become plentiful and cheap enough for it to dominate long case clock design. Only from about 1760 onwards were mahogany grandfather clocks made in sufficient quantities for generalizations regarding typical design. After that, mahogany was often used for the carcases, too; this might be veneered with figured mahogany, inlaid with other woods such as satin-wood and holly, or patterned with the type of marquetry associated with the Adam period. Oak and pine carcases were also largely used but only in the plentiful country work was the oak left without veneer.

Because they were designed for magnificent high-ceilinged rooms, clocks of the mahogany period were of the broader, heavier build required to balance arched dial and towering hood. In country work, for less lofty apartments, the case designer compromised with wide but shorter body and dumpy base, some Yorkshire work being particularly broad-waisted. These country clocks require special consideration because they displayed various characteristics associated with earlier work. Many followed the earlier design with small single-handed dials, square-topped like their body-doors; their decoration consisted of little more than clumsy inlay and the country workman's typical attempt at gentility, oak banded with mahogany. While the finer long case clocks had eight-day movements (month, three-month, and year movements were sometimes devised) this type often retained the old thirty-hour mechanism and might be wound by pulling up the single weight instead of being fitted with two weights and the customary winding equipment.

In better quality work the typical hood was a heavily handsome structure, the cornice arched, topped with a broken pediment or otherwise elaborated and set off by corner and central finials. There was distinctive use of mouldings and sometimes a considerable amount of fret-cut and card-cut work in cresting and frieze. Only in north country products, however, was there much use of carving —a notable feature of many Lancashire and Cheshire clocks. Such fantasies as "French" rococo details, "Chinese" pagoda-shaped hoods and "Gothic" arches, pillars, and cluster columns reflected the various trends of the period, with appropriate treatment of body and base. Sometimes the hood was given extra width by duplication of the side pillars; often the body door was flanked by two pillars or by reeded pilasters set in the splayed corners. The base might have its front corners similarly splayed—additional ground for classic inlay during the late years of the century.

Chippendale is believed to have based some of his clock case designs on the work of the Huguenot Daniel Marot, published in Amsterdam in 1712. Those in his French rococo style were overpoweringly flamboyant, their decoration including ornate ormolu mounts.

Dials at this period might still be in the old brass tradition, their arches enlivened with such moving figures as Father Time, ships on the sea, boxers, and so on. But by about 1755 still greater clarity was being achieved with a dial made in one piece, including the hour ring and spandrels, and completely silvered. On these dials the spandrels were finely engraved, but this was essentially a price-cutting idea and during George III's reign workmanship deteriorated. There was considerable overlapping in the use of various dial media, and many high quality dials still had attached gilded spandrels, often engraved after casting, while cheaper clocks showed rough, unfinished castings. Spandrel decoration included a crown and crossed sceptres among scrolling foliage and various rococo devices, engraved and pierced.

Soon after the mid-century, too, dials of white enamel were being produced: they had been used for watches in the seventeenth century but remained comparatively rare on long case clocks. Dossie, in *The Handmaid to the Arts* (1758), said, "The white glass made at Mr. Bowle's glass-house in Southwark, is frequently used for the grounds of enamel dial-plates", and praised its low price and great whiteness; the use of japanning for such a purpose was a later development, for at this time no base had been found for the varnish which did not spoil the whiteness of the dial. Enamelled or painted dials might have their arches and spandrel corners imaginatively decorated with all kinds of pictorial motifs such as the four seasons, the continents, Biblical scenes, and so on, and it was these that were imitated in inferior work on the many cheap clocks of the late eighteenth century with smaller square faces painted on iron or wood.

In general, the trend was ever towards a greater concentration on the lower price market—even to the inclusion of clocks in painted, soft-wood cases. Some clocks of Sheraton's day were of fine workmanship, expressing the period's love of satin-wood and other beautiful veneers and various more or less classical devices in inlay and marquetry: Sheraton's

Drawing Book (1793) illustrated two extremely ornate examples with figure medallions on the body doors. But already the grandfather was going out of fashion, and indeed in his *Dictionary* (1803) Sheraton called it "almost obsolete in London".

To-day, collectors particularly cherish those grandfathers in which the early master designers achieved grace, proportion, and perfect clarity—and perhaps most of all the diminutive "grandmother" clock, only five to six feet tall, rare and wholly charming.

INDEX

Note: References to diagrams in the text are in bold type.